The
Spiritual Exercises
of ECK

This book has been authored by and published under the supervision of the Living ECK Master, Sri Harold Klemp. It is the Word of ECK.

The Spiritual Exercises of ECK

Harold Klemp

ECKANKAR
Minneapolis, MN

The Spiritual Exercises of ECK

The terms ECKANKAR, ECK, EK, MAHANTA, SOUL TRAVEL, and VAIRAGI, among others, are trademarks of ECKANKAR, P.O. Box 27300, Minneapolis, MN 55427 U.S.A.

Printed in U.S.A.

With grateful acknowledgment to Myrtis Affeld, James Davis, and Charlie Siegel for their loving contributions in the preparation of this book.

Compiled by Mary Carroll Moore
Edited by Joan Klemp and Anthony Moore

Cover design by Doug Munson
Cover illustration by Phil Morimitsu
Text illustrations by Catherine Purnell
Text photo (page xiv) by Robert Huntley
Back cover photo by Bree Renz

Second Printing—1994

Library of Congress Cataloging-in-Publication Data
Klemp, Harold.
    The spiritual exercises of ECK / Harold Klemp
      p. cm.
    Includes bibliographical references.
    ISBN 1-57043-001-2
    1. Eckankar (Organization) 2. Spiritual exercises. I. Title.
BP605.E3K574 1993
299' .93—dc20
                                  93-31410
                                       CIP

The Spiritual Exercises of ECK in this book are those made public by the Mahanta, the Living ECK Master in books, publications, and seminar talks. It does not include the more specialized spiritual exercises given by the Living ECK Master in his discourses to members of ECKANKAR.

The Spiritual Exercises of ECK are a treasure whose value we might overlook because of their simplicity. But they are your lifeline to the Word of God. The Mahanta has put this key to higher states of consciousness in your hand.

—Sri Harold Klemp

Contents

Chapter Three: Healing and Protection

Chapter Four: Exercises for Balance
and Harmony

Chapter Twelve: Troubleshooting the
Spiritual Exercises of ECK

Sri Harold Klemp at the 1992 ECK Summer Festival in Anaheim, California. As the Mahanta, the Living ECK Master his mission is to help others find the doorway to freedom, wisdom, and love through the daily Spiritual Exercises of ECKANKAR.

Foreword

Since the dawn of history, people have yearned to touch the heart of God. They have tried many ways to do it: worship, prayer, meditation, contemplation, invocation, chanting, and singing.

These methods have stood the test of time, in the sense that they are still widely used around the world. But have they stood the test of lifting the seeker up to God?

No doubt all methods uplift the seeker to some level. But there is one difference between the Spiritual Exercises of ECKANKAR and the practices of other religions. Whosoever does the Spiritual Exercises of ECK faithfully can reach the kingdom of heaven while still in the physical body.

No matter who you are, no matter how good or bad you think you are, you are a unique individual. Soul, both in Its being and in Its relationship with God, is unique. If you are ready, the Spiritual Exercises of ECK can help you find your own custom-made approach to God.

These spiritual exercises link you with the guidance of the Holy Spirit, which is seen as Light and heard as Sound.

Chapter One

Starting with the Spiritual Exercises of ECK

When you step onto the path to God and you begin looking for that secret path to heaven, the way will be opened for you. And the way lies through the Spiritual Exercises of ECK.

These spiritual exercises link you with the guidance of the Holy Spirit, which is seen as Light and heard as Sound. The inner Sound is the Voice of God calling us home. The inner Light is a beacon to light our way. All the Spiritual Exercises of ECK are built on these two divine aspects of the Holy Spirit.

Learning spiritual consciousness is learning how to live in this world no matter what comes. We learn through these spiritual exercises how to live life graciously, from childhood to old age. We learn how to live life in the best way possible.

The Spiritual Exercises of ECK give us confidence in ourselves. We learn that we are Soul, we are eternal. Then we know with certainty that we live forever, that death cannot destroy us.

You can do the spiritual exercises in a number of different ways. Usually, any guidelines I give are to help you develop the self-discipline to remember what's happening on the inner planes.

When you do the Spiritual Exercises of ECK, fill yourself with love and goodwill. Then say,

"I now put my inner experience into your hands, Mahanta. Take me wherever is best for my own unfoldment at this particular time."

You can train yourself to remember, if you keep a notebook handy. It's hard, but that's what I did. Train yourself to wake up in the middle of the night and write down an experience. As you develop the discipline of remembering inner experiences, you also develop the strength to handle them.

Be patient with yourself. It is a rare person who has instant success and dramatic results right away. Expect subtle, gradual changes in your outlook on life over a period of weeks or months. A good way to keep track of this is by using a journal to note any insights, perceptions, or changes you notice in yourself.

Use the spiritual exercise that works best for you based on the outer conditions you're faced with. No matter which one you use, all you really want is experience with the Light and Sound of God.

Do one exercise every day. Spend about twenty minutes on it. This builds your spiritual stamina gently over time. Regular daily practice is the key to success.

1. Dreams, Soul Travel, and Love

There are many ECK spiritual exercises. Each one opens you a little bit more to the Sound and Light of God.

This spiritual exercise is for three different groups of people: (1) those who don't dream but want to, (2) those who dream but want to Soul Travel, and (3) those who want to go beyond dreams and Soul Travel to the state of direct knowingness. The exercise is so simple that it may seem as if I'm belittling your intelligence, but I'm not. Truth is always simple.

Just before you go to sleep, sit quietly on your bed. Close your eyes. Chant HU very softly, or if someone is in the room with you, chant it silently to yourself. HU is a special word, the ancient name for God. You could call it the manifested Word or the Sound; it has a power of its own.

As you take the time to sit there and chant HU, the name of God, you are making a commitment with Divine Spirit. Chant HU in a long, drawn-out way for three or four or five minutes, and let yourself settle down. Then wait for a few more minutes before starting the next step.

For those who have been unable to remember their dreams, simply chant the word *dream* spelled out. Chant it out loud, letter by letter: D-R-E-A-M. Do this for about five minutes. Next, chant the same thing quietly for a few minutes, and then just go to sleep. As you are falling asleep, say, "I would like to remember a significant spiritual dream." With this method, you are asking for truth to come through the dream state.

Some of you want Soul Travel, which is usually an advanced state beyond the dream state. Again, sit on your bed or on the floor, shut your eyes, and look into your Spiritual Eye. This is located at a point just above and between the eyebrows. Don't expect to see anything there; just chant HU, the holy name of God.

Then spell out *Soul Travel,* chanting each separate letter: S-O-U-L T-R-A-V-E-L. Do this about three times out loud and then three times quietly.

Those who have Soul traveled may now want to go to the higher state of direct knowingness, without having to go through the intermediary stages. Dreams and Soul Travel are helpful and important, but at some point you outgrow them.

Simply chant the words *divine love.* Originally I was going to give it as L-O-V-E, but some people would mix it up with human love. The word *divine* takes it beyond human love. Divine love brings you all forms of love, including human love. To limit it to the usual definition of love is like working from the bottom, instead of working from the top of spirituality.

So, chant D-I-V-I-N-E L-O-V-E. This means you seek the highest form of love, which brings all blessings to you.

2. Listening for God

Try this simple spiritual exercise to help you hear and see the two aspects of God, the Light and Sound.

Go somewhere quiet. Sit or lie down in a comfortable place. Put your attention on your Spiritual Eye, a point just above and behind your eyebrows. With eyes lightly shut, begin to sing a holy word or phrase, such as HU, God, Holy Spirit, or "Show me thy Ways, O Lord." But fill your heart with love before you approach the altar of God, because only the pure may come.

Be patient. Do this exercise for several weeks, for a limit of twenty minutes each time. Sit, sing, and wait. God speaks to you only when you are able to listen.

3. Taking a Spiritual Break

If there is any moment during the day where you need a little boost, declare yourself a vehicle for God. It'll help you through a lot of things.

If you want to bring yourself closer to the ECK, say, "I am a vehicle for the SUGMAD, the ECK, and the Mahanta." Then begin your day with joy. Know that everything is being accomplished as it should be.

If things seem too much for you, you can also close your eyes for a moment and imagine yourself taking a golden spiritual shower. The shower is of the Light of ECK. Imagine standing beneath this stream of Light which is bringing you surrender through divine love.

And remember, you can get through the biggest things if you go moment by moment.

4. Count Your Blessings

An ECK Higher Initiate wanted to be more open to love. He asked me if there was a special technique for greater surrender that would bring this about.

There is a technique, but unlike other spiritual exercises, it does not have a beginning, middle, and end. This technique involves attitude, and it is one that must be lived. In a word, it's called *gratitude*.

Throughout the day, contemplate on all the blessings in your life. The power of gratitude opens the heart to allow love to enter. But once the love comes in and we receive the gifts of Divine Spirit and of life, the way to keep the gifts flowing is to be grateful.

5. Show Me Love

If you don't know anything about ECK, the main tool you have to work with at this point may be prayer—your communication with God. If you are sincerely interested in truth, in knowing who you are and why you belong here, ask God in your prayers: "Show me truth."

If your heart is pure, the Lord will bring truth into your life. But don't expect it to come in a way that fits your expectations; it may come in a different way. It may come through the gift of a book or by way of a person telling you one small step that you need to take before you can go to the next step.

And so you can pray to God. Just say, "I want truth," or "Dear Lord, give me knowledge, wisdom, and understanding." But the greatest thing you could ask is: "Dear Lord, give me love."

Knowledge, wisdom, and understanding are only the attributes of God. But when you have love, you have the whole thing. We seek first the highest, most divine, most sacred part of something which is nothing other than our own inner being. And with this come the attributes of God and the spiritual liberation, which is something no baptism can ever bring.

When you ask for truth with a pure heart, Divine Spirit will take you one step closer to coming home to God.

6. Combining Contemplation and Dreams

A simple method of moving into the higher states of awareness is to combine contemplation and dreams. Find a quiet place for contemplation.

For a period of fifteen or twenty minutes a day, shut your eyes and put attention upon your Spiritual Eye. This is the spiritual organ of inner vision. It sits between the eyebrows, about an inch and a half in.

Look gently at an imaginary screen between the eyebrows and softly begin to sing *Jesus, God, HU,* or *Mahanta. Wah Z* is also acceptable.

Look for a Blue Light upon the inner screen. This is the Light of God. There may not be this Light, but you may hear a Sound. The Sound is the other manifestation of the ECK, or Holy Spirit. It can be almost any sound of nature or musical instrument that you can imagine. The Light and Sound, when they appear, are assurance of your contact with the Word of God.

The second part of this exercise is for the dream state. Prepare for sleep by singing one of the words given above. This is to set into motion an affinity with the Sound Current, the Holy Spirit. For a few minutes, sing the word you have chosen. When you are ready for sleep, imagine that you are walking in a park or watching a quiet sunset with someone you love.

A loved one can open our heart and dispel any fear. Love is necessary if one is to enter the awakened dream state.

Finally, keep a diary of whatever comes to mind in contemplation or during your dream state. A mutual confidence will develop between your inner and outer selves, and the two techniques above will help accomplish that.

This is a good way to start the dream teachings of ECK.

The experiences you have will lead to greater awareness of your life and its divine meaning.

Chapter Two

Dream Exercises

7. Inviting the Dream Master

The Dream Master, who is really the Living ECK Master, will not work with the dreamer unless invited in some way.

Before going to sleep, inwardly give permission to the Dream Master to be with you. Imagine unburdening yourself, giving your problems to him, and letting your mind relax its concerns and worries. Ask the Dream Master to help clear up the karmic conditions of whatever is standing in the way of your spiritual growth.

Then go to sleep, aware that you are resting in the care of the Dream Master who will look out for your best interests.

8. The Golden Cup

Every evening at bedtime, visualize a golden cup to be filled with your dream experiences. The cup sits by your bed. When you awake in the morning, in contemplation or in your imagination, drink from the cup. You are drinking in the experiences, a conscious way of saying, I want to remember what I'm doing on the inner planes while my body is asleep.

The golden cup is Soul; it is you. As you put more attention on drinking from the cup, it takes on a life of its own. The more the ECK flows in and out of the cup, the more Soul shines of Its own golden light. You, as Soul, become an ever-brighter vehicle for the Holy Spirit.

The experiences you have will lead to greater awareness of your life and its divine meaning.

9. The Dream Dictionary

During important times in my life, one of the dream symbols I used to see was a field with a regular-sized baseball diamond. When everything on the field was aligned and in proper order—four bases evenly spaced, a pitcher, a batter, and two opposing teams—it meant that my life was in good order.

But sometimes the bases were at odd distances apart or the base path wasn't in a perfect square. Or the ball I'd hit might pop and blow feathers all over the place. Or I'd have to run into the woods to find first base. Second base might be closer in than usual; third base might be off in another direction entirely. In other words, everything about the game was wrong.

When I'd wake up after a dream like that, I'd often notice that something in my outer life wasn't going right. The sport had gone out of it. There wasn't any fun in it.

This was an indication for me to sit down and work out a plan to reorganize. In other words, I had to figure out how to get myself a real baseball field again—proper space between bases, correct number of players on each team, and so on.

Creating a dream dictionary can help you become familiar with your own dream symbols. Whether a baseball diamond, a bear, an eagle, or anything else, you'll know immediately what a particular symbol means to you.

In a section at the back of your dream journal, keep a list of the symbols that occur in your dreams. As you create your own dream dictionary of symbols, record the date next to the meaning of each symbol. This way you can keep track as the meaning changes. As you unfold, your dream symbols are going to take on different meanings, a fact not generally known by people who study dreams.

10. Door of Soul

The door of Soul opens inwardly. No amount of pushing from the wrong side will open it. For this reason, twenty minutes to half an hour is the limit of time to spend with the spiritual exercises during one sitting.

To have an experience with the Light and Sound of God or the Inner Master, alternate these two techniques:

1. Count backward slowly from ten to one, then picture yourself standing alongside your resting physical body. Do this for a few weeks. You may also recite the alphabet backward from J to A.

2. Do the second method when you've finished contemplation and are getting ready for bed. Say inwardly to the Dream Master, the Mahanta, "I give you permission to take me into the Far Country, to the place that is right for me now."

Then go to sleep without giving the thought command another bit of attention. The command unlocks the unconscious so the experiences of Soul can be retained by the human mind.

Keep a notebook within easy reach to make notes.

Remember that spiritually things work without pushing. When you have ECK in your life, it's not necessary to push.

27

11. Learning about Surrender

During contemplation, declare yourself an instrument of love for the SUGMAD (God), the ECK, and the Mahanta. Softly sing HU for several minutes. You may hear the Sound as a buzz or pulse like an electrical current. This is one of the many sounds of the Holy Spirit.

If the Sound is loud and stays with you after contemplation, making you restless and unable to sleep, ask the Dream Master, "How can I surrender to the Sound of God?"

Imagine the Dream Master telling you he will teach you about surrender in the dream state tonight. He instructs you to first still your thoughts, then repeat to yourself the phrase, "I surrender to the ECK."

In the morning write down your dreams, and take them into contemplation. What did you learn about surrender?

12. Dreaming Consciously

To learn to move consciously into a new or higher plane in the dream state, try this technique.

Before sleep gently place the attention on the Living ECK Master. In your dream state, return your attention to the Living ECK Master, who will appear as the Dream Master.

In your dream, anchor your attention on some solid object in the room. While you are focused, give yourself this thought command, I am awakening in my dream. As you anchor your attention on the object as a point of concentration, you will find yourself rising as if through veils of consciousness. You will move into a new plane just as solid as the physical.

If you fail to maintain your concentration on the object in the dream, you will sink into the dream state and awaken in a natural way.

During the dream you can also put yourself in the position of a silent witness, watching others enact their roles, much as you watch a movie. You can learn to start and stop the dream, make the dream bright or dim, in color or black and white.

Another way to dream consciously is to practice watching yourself drop off to sleep each night. Learn to catch that point where you dip into the larger reservoir of the dream state.

Through practice you can learn to rest the body and be in a conscious state of awareness. You can do this without fear. You can then learn to move from one dream level to another, without losing consciousness.

The question always arises: What should I do if I am consciously dreaming or on a different plane and I want to get back into the awareness of the physical body? There is one basic rule: Assume with the sense of feeling that you are in your physical body. This will happen immediately.

13. Dream Characters

Human characters play leading parts in most dreams. They are often people who are close to us in everyday life. In many cases, they represent other things than themselves.

Most dreamers can learn their own feelings or thoughts about a person by studying what the dream character does or says.

If you wish to use this technique, write down not only the dream upon awakening but also your thoughts and feelings about it and the people you encountered.

14. Getting Answers in Dreams

At some level Soul knows everything. If there is something that you would like to bring into consciousness, here is a way to get help.

Before you go to sleep, relax and decide that upon awakening you will have an answer to whatever it is that you desire.

When you awaken it will be in the forefront of your thoughts. At the moment of slipping from or into sleep, you are opened to truth and in direct contact with it. It is at this point that you will perceive your answer.

Immediately make note of it in your dream journal.

We know that there is an answer for every situation that comes up in our life. There is always a way, somehow. What holds us back is our attitudes.

Learn the value of doing a spiritual exercise just before retiring or upon awakening. It works to your advantage during these times of change in conscious awareness.

15. The Formula Technique

Like so many other ECKists, I found that when I went into contemplation or the dream state, I'd have an experience on the inner planes. But I often wondered, How can I tell whether the experience happened on the Astral Plane, the Causal Plane, or the Mental Plane?

I knew there was a difference between these levels, but when something occurred, I often couldn't tell where it came from.

One night the ECK Master Peddar Zaskq gave me a technique. "It's like a visitor's pass to the other planes," he told me. "Anyone can use it, whether you're a First Initiate or a Fourth. Instead of just letting the experience happen and then hoping someone will show you a sign that tells you in bright letters where you are, you have a way to tell where you are in the inner worlds."

Formula Two works for visiting the Astral Plane. You chant HU two times, then you breathe two times. You keep doing this for fifteen minutes, before bed or in contemplation. Lightly keep in mind that you want to visit the Astral Plane.

Formula Three works for the Causal Plane; it's the same procedure, except you chant three times and breathe three times. This is the plane of seed ideas and seed karma. When you go to sleep you very gently try to hold thoughts of the Causal Plane.

Formula Four is for the Mental Plane; you chant HU four times, then breathe four times. Formula Five is for the Soul Plane: five HUs and five breaths.

Before you begin, write in your dream journal which formula you are going to try. After you have any degree of success with this, begin comparing all the experiences of the same plane. See if there isn't a thread that works through them. There is a different texture to all the experiences on the Astral level than there is for the Causal, where you're trying to see past lives.

I found this technique very helpful. Perhaps you can try it tonight or in the weeks to come.

16. Dream Book

The first rule in keeping a dream book is to write simply. Writing complex ideas in everyday language is hard work. A dream may have so many details in it that you can become sidetracked from the point.

To overcome this, write the dream out in full. Then put it away. At the end of the month, review those inner experiences that stand out. Condense them. Make believe you are an editor on the staff of *Reader's Digest*.

Gather the best of your experiences and send them to the Living ECK Master in a report. If you are an ECK initiate, this can be your initiate report. It is an easy way to resolve karma.

17. Nap Time

You can begin to study dreams during a nap. When you feel tired, set an alarm for twenty minutes. Have a notebook handy; this will be your dream book.

Put your attention upon the Mahanta, the Living ECK Master; but do this in a light, easy way—almost as an afterthought.

Now tell yourself that you will have a peaceful nap and that you will remember a little of what occurs in the other worlds when you awaken. Then go to sleep.

When the alarm rings, jot down whatever you can remember, no matter how foolish it seems. In time, you may expand your study of dreams; this method is easy to do even in a busy family.

18. Journey on an Ocean of Light

Tonight when you go to bed, close your eyes and locate the Spiritual Eye. It is at a point right above and between the eyebrows. Now very gently look for the Light, which can come in a number of different ways.

At first you may see just a general glow of light that you think is merely your imagination. It might appear as little blue spots of light or as a ray of light. Or it could look like a beam of light coming through an open window from the sunshine outside. The white light may also show up in any number of ways.

As you look for the Light, chant your secret word or HU, a name for God which has a power greater than the word *God* for many people. Watch as this Light turns into an ocean of light. Then, as you see It turn into an ocean, look for a little boat that's coming to shore very near where you are standing. At the helm is the Mahanta or one of the ECK Masters, who will invite you into the boat. Don't be afraid; just get in.

When you get to this point, allow any experience to follow that may. Set no limitations on it. You may end up in a video arcade, or you may end up near or inside a Temple of Golden Wisdom. Or you may have an experience of the Light and Sound of God coming directly into Soul.

19. Mahanta, I Love You

This spiritual exercise can be done while falling asleep, silently chanting HU or your personal word.

Start with a simple postulate, something very open and easy such as, "Mahanta, I love you." Then quietly, in the background of the mind, begin to sing HU. Just let it run on spiritual automatic. But automatic doesn't mean letting it turn into a meaningless mental repetition. Rather, in a very real sense, you remain conscious that the HU is rolling within you.

If you wake up in the middle of the night, you can spiritualize your consciousness by briefly putting your attention on the Mahanta, even for a second or two.

Know that you do this because you love God. You love the divine part within yourself. In this gentle, unpushy way, you become the lover of all life.

20. Watching Yourself Fall Asleep

Every night before retiring, relax on the bed. Watch the process of going to sleep. Keep your attention on the point between the eyebrows, the Spiritual Eye.

As your body relaxes and your mind settles down, that change in viewpoint takes place which we call sleep. Maintain the attitude of awareness. You will note your body getting quiet and your thoughts settling down. Hearing is often the last to leave the human consciousness. You will be detached on the borderline state, as though in a dream.

Then you will come into another state of beingness. This is characterized by a clarity of mental vision. It is not an unconscious state like a mental fog, but a level of awareness beyond the limits of normal human expression.

This viewpoint may last a moment or for several hours. With practice it may last through the whole night.

To hold on to this lucidity, you need to maintain a delicate balance between not becoming too emotional and not forgetting that you are dreaming.

What has happened? As the body rests, you awaken in the Atma Sarup, the Soul body. You find yourself in eternity, overcoming death. This is the freedom which is spoken about so often in ECKANKAR.

21. Seminar Dreams

Sometimes you will find yourself working on the inner planes in settings very much as we find at an ECKANKAR seminar. Maybe you are acting as an usher, working in the higher worlds.

You are carrying out some act of service to the ECK out of love. You act out of love for that Sound and Light of God which has filled you.

To attend an ECKANKAR seminar inwardly, do this: Before sleep go into contemplation and visualize whatever you can about the seminar, using the description you've read in the preregistration brochure. Put yourself on the inner planes and say, "I am seeing myself with my friends at the ECK seminar. I'm seeing myself in the audience listening to the Master."

If you wish to consciously serve in this way, give yourself a silent command before sleep. Then let the matter rest in the hands of Divine Spirit.

The healing Light of God will start to uplift you from the materialism and karma that you have created for yourself through ignorance of God's laws.

Chapter Three

Healing and Protection

22. Using Light for Healing

In your spiritual exercises there are two things you can use for healing. One is the orange light, and the other is the blue light. You may wish to experiment with them. Some people are successful in this kind of healing, and others are better off seeing a doctor. It depends on you.

The orange light is mostly for the physical body. Go into contemplation in your usual way, whether you sit up or lie down. Using the imaginative power, which is the God force or the seeing power of Soul, shut your eyes and visualize the Audible Life Stream. This is the pure white Light of God, a composite of all the colors.

Now visualize a ray coming off of It. It's very much like using a prism to see the spectrum of colors.

The ray you see is orange, which applies to physical health. With your eyes closed, visualize this orange stream coming through you. Just let it flow to the area in your body that is diseased, afflicted, or injured. You can do this for twenty minutes.

This is a healing technique. But you do it only for yourself; don't go out and blast orange light at other people.

The blue light is another way of healing, but it is for the inner bodies—the Astral, Causal,

Mental, and Etheric. These are the bodies of the psychic worlds below the Soul Plane.

Here again, you use a technique similar to that of the orange light. And I'll repeat this: Do it only for yourself, never for another person.

Close your eyes and visualize the blue light coming into the heart center. This light is known as the Blue Light of the Mahanta. The Mahanta Consciousness is the highest state of consciousness known to man. The blue light is for the calming and healing of the inner man—your emotions and your mind. Along with this technique, get plenty of physical rest.

The blue light is not something that is created out of the ethers from some source alien to yourself. It comes from your own God Worlds, and you are now becoming aware of it.

Let this healing Light of God come in and work on the area you feel needs help. Or just let It flow into the Spiritual Eye. As It washes and cleanses the impurities, It will start to uplift you from the materialism and karma that you have created for yourself through ignorance of God's laws.

A true spiritual healing first heals the spiritual condition that caused the symptoms to appear in the physical body. You have to understand that when you use the orange light, it may not bring a miraculous healing, such as the reshaping of limbs, or anything like this. But it may lead you to a better doctor.

23. The Mountain of Light

Try this if you feel you are in need of spiritual protection. Shut your eyes at bedtime, and see yourself standing before a gigantic mountain of light. From the mountain flows the most enchanting melody of the Audible Life Stream.

Now visualize yourself walking up the sidewalk to the huge door that guards the entrance into the side of the mountain. The door's mighty construction can withstand a thermonuclear blast.

Pull the door shut behind you. Notice how easily it swings, despite its great height and massive construction. With the door shut and you safely inside the shelter, lock the door securely. Snap the padlock, set the dead bolt, and drop the bar into place. Then turn around and walk directly into the worlds of Light and Sound behind you.

In extreme cases, it is perfectly all right to create several outer chambers inside the entrance. Each chamber is likewise protected by an enormous door; all are secured against the night.

Be aware of one thing: the door of protection is made from the ECK Itself. Nothing can get through it!

I can help you—but only if you listen. Nothing can hurt you spiritually, unless you yourself allow it.

24. The Sound Room

Go into contemplation and find yourself on the inner planes with Wah Z, the Inner Master. He takes you to a room in a beautiful Temple of Golden Wisdom. He says, "This is the sound room. Would you like a sound healing?" You say, "Sure."

He tells you to climb on the big stone table in the center of the room. As you lie there, the Sound currents of ECK begin massaging your inner bodies. This relaxes you, and the transformation begins. After a little while you feel the Sound Current raise you off the table toward the ceiling. You pass through a small opening into higher states, where the Sound Current is much more refined.

Feel your troubles or pain gradually leave you until they are all gone. Then come out of contemplation.

When the healing occurs, it brings balance to the inner bodies. It may take some time to filter to the physical, and your life tomorrow might not be easier than it was today. But at least now you know about the sound room at the Temple of Golden Wisdom and can ask to go there whenever you need to.

25. A Way to Build Self-Confidence

If you should have your real strength of character marred by a lack of self-confidence, use this technique to build yourself up again.

First find the spots in your aura or personal atmosphere that are self-conscious, shy, timid, or overly sensitive. These tend to attract people who impose upon your weakness. With a mental command, ask those people to move out of your way. Mentally demand respectful attention.

Next build up the opposite qualities of mind and character to replace these self-conscious qualities. Fill yourself with positive courage so that the positive force you generate can actually be felt when you pass through a room.

Adopt the mental attitude and personal atmosphere of a person with great confidence. Always be direct and positive in your approach to all things. Put all your spiritual force behind your smile, your replies, and your thoughts.

26. Spiritual Strength in Hard Times

Through the hard times and the happy times, wherever you are and whatever you are doing, you need only place your attention on the Mahanta to know that the Master is with you.

This spiritual exercise of putting your attention on the Mahanta will help you develop a surety of strength as you become Higher Initiates and eventually ECK Masters. You will have what you need to go anywhere in life, anywhere on earth, and anywhere in the planes of God.

Then sing HU, a special name for God. When you sing HU, you agree to let Divine Spirit do what is best for you. Singing HU does not guarantee a healing, but it does arrange for the conditions that are best for spiritual unfoldment.

27. Defense against Black Magic

The forces of black magic are powerful in Africa. ECKists there ask me, How can we become strong so that no force of Kal, the negative power, can harm us?

First, do not look for trouble or anger anyone who has these powers. But if the powers of darkness are thrown against you, put your full attention on the Mahanta and sing, or chant, HU. See a shining light around you through which no evil can penetrate, and know that the Mahanta in the form of a Blue Light stands by your side.

Study what *The Shariyat* says about how to overcome the dark forces. It is important to understand what in your emotions has opened the door for this power to attack.

Always remember that the ECK is stronger than any force in the lower worlds. Only one who surrounds himself with Its presence, and knows that the Mahanta is with him, will be safe.

28. Techniques for Protection

To survive a psychic attack one may take several approaches:

1. A conscious closing of the emotional door against the intruder. Any photos, as well as memorabilia, of a disruptive personality must be put out of the house.
2. The constant chanting of HU or the initiate's personal word.
3. An actual fight on the inner planes whereby the trespasser is driven off by martial arts or some weapon at hand.
4. Getting plenty of rest each night.

The old law of protection is this: Nothing can hurt us unless we ourselves allow it. People under psychic attack must make a decision whether to follow the Lord of Light and Sound or the lord of darkness.

Hesitation creates a split current of energy within one. I've had reports of people who suffered heart attacks because they let their emotions pull them in two different directions at the same time. Forgo the worship of Moloch, the worship of personality. The price is too dear.

29. Declaration

You will find this declaration useful as a protection:

I declare myself a vehicle for the SUGMAD.

Wait a brief moment while you feel the stream of SUGMAD enter your being. It is a certain distinctive force.

I declare myself a vehicle for the SUGMAD and the ECK.

And then wait a moment until this flow of ECK fills Soul. You'll feel an entirely different current come through.

I declare myself a vehicle for the SUGMAD, the ECK, and the Mahanta.

Again, still another energy comes through, this one happy and light, like a little lamb dancing along on musical feet.

This is the consciousness that can help you relate to people, in an everyday way, a connection to the high principles of ECK and the SUGMAD.

Then go forth to meet your day with confidence, because the Mahanta is always with you.

30. Restoring Harmony

Whenever somebody is making it difficult for you at work, simply sing HU quietly to yourself. Let the other person vent his rage, and just wait and see what the ECK will do to work out the situation.

You'll find that you know what to say or not to say, when to speak or be quiet, when and how to keep out of the individual's way, or whether it will be necessary to appeal to the person's supervisor to get him off your back.

When you run into these things, by all means sing HU to open yourself as a channel for God. You don't use the HU to change the other person's state of consciousness; you use it for your protection.

It surrounds you with a blanket of white light, and whatever is thrown at you must return to the sender. The person who attacks you often finds himself so busy with his own problems that he no longer has time to continue his attacks on you.

31. The Living ECK Master's Image

In your inner vision, put the image of the Living ECK Master in front of you like a screen. Imagine that all thoughts, words, actions, and feelings flowing from you must pass through this screen. Likewise, all things coming toward you must pass through the image of the Master.

A chela who tried this exercise wrote, "I was given a job to do at work. Within two hours I felt shaky and got upset. Then I remembered you had said to hold your image in mind and let you do for me. Within thirty minutes I had completed the job and put the papers on my employer's desk. He congratulated me for my efficiency and industry."

The image of the Living ECK Master acts as the matrix for the Holy Spirit to come flowing through, lifting you into the higher planes, and giving you greater love.

32. Calling Upon the Little People

If you find yourself in a situation where you sense danger, use your imagination in contemplation to repair the situation. Rather than giving up to the hand of fear, call upon the little people.

If you are on an airplane, for example, you can imagine a force of neatly uniformed little workers tightening all the rivets, bolts, and nuts. See them making sure all the hoses and nozzles are secured. Once you set the scenario in motion in your imagination, it will take over. All you have to do is watch them work.

Whenever there is a crisis, you can work with creative exercises and visualize workers fixing whatever is wrong. It isn't limited to airplanes; it can be done anywhere, even in your office.

But be careful not to visualize workers beating up your boss or co-workers who won't do something your way. That puts you in the field of power. In some way you will pay for power: things will go wrong and backfire on you.

You don't have to passively accept what the Lords of Karma hand out as your lot in life. If a warning comes on the inner that something negative is about to happen, you can use your creative imagination. Know that there is a way to neutralize that experience—if it is the will of the ECK.

33. Shield of Silver Light

In the forest of the SUGMAD is an enormous clearing. It is set in a breathtakingly beautiful landscape, where the sky is baby blue, speckled with fluffy white clouds.

Against the stump of an ancient tree, all by itself in the middle of the clearing, stands a silver shield. It appears as a mighty warrior's shield from medieval times. The Light of God shines down from above, strikes the shield, and comes off in a ray of light so brilliant that it will blind anyone who approaches it with an impure heart.

This Shield of Silver Light stands as a protection for the children of ECK, those who make the commitment to follow the shield of love. No being can approach it except in the spirit of love. And when you can approach the Shield of Silver Light in the spirit of love, you have the protection of the Mahanta with you. Nothing can touch you, nothing can harm you.

When battle must be done to bring protection to Its own, the Inner Master, the Mahanta, will go to the clearing, pick up the shield, and with the sword of the SUGMAD he will take the field in battle for you.

If you know and accept this, then you have the love and protection of the Holy Spirit against every psychic attack, against all harm and all danger. In times of danger, you have the ability to wrap this aura of love so tightly about you that nothing can touch you.

In your contemplation, see yourself walking beside the Mahanta through the meadows to this great forest. When you reach the clearing in the middle of the forest, you will find the Shield of Silver Light, which is the shield of love. Stand within its circle of protection, and know that you are standing in the love and protection of the SUGMAD.

34. Self-Protection

To protect yourself you must remember two principles: (1) never believe that you will be harmed by anything or anybody, because you are ageless, eternal Soul; and (2) practice fearlessness by never being afraid of anything or letting the imagination run wild by imagining something happening to your body to harm it.

Three techniques for self-protection are: (1) place a reversed mirror in front of you, which the adversary's psychic self can see but cannot withstand; (2) place a white light around yourself; and (3) start talking in a normal voice, telling your adversary that he isn't acting according to the laws of human decency.

35. Reversing a Bad Dream

When you have a bad dream and wake up afraid or angry, you can imagine yourself changing the dream's ending.

For instance, if you dream you are in a dark building, imagine walking out of the building into the sunlight. Imagine yourself moving from a lower, darker world into a higher, lighter one. When you do this, you may suddenly understand the meaning of the dream.

36. Wah Z!

Some people think imagining the Mahanta nearby is just an empty fantasy, but it's not. We couldn't imagine something unless there was a reality to it.

If you need help or protection, call out for Wah Z and visualize him standing near you. Wah Z is the name by which the present Living ECK Master is known in the spiritual sense. Or you can simply use the name Z, which is an abbreviated form.

Then just relax and know that help is near. The Inner Master, the Mahanta, will be working with you to bring the experience that is important for you now.

As quickly as we can release our attachment to whatever is hurting us, the karma can pass off. This way we stay balanced.

Chapter Four

Exercises for Balance and Harmony

37. Avoiding Daily Karma

As karma surfaces, it works out through the weakest point in our body. As quickly as we can release our attachment to whatever is hurting us, the karma can pass off. This way we stay balanced.

When I was a chela in ECK, the Master once showed me how to make less daily karma. He stressed the importance of words in everyday speech. Comparative words such as *almost, nearly,* and *pretty near* used too often make us seem indecisive to the people we live and work with.

I began to substitute more direct speech.

He also told me that the overuse of demanding words such as *should, ought,* and *must* belong in the vocabulary of a person who desires control over others. People sense that and shy away from him. That aversion is karma.

Thereafter I began the process of learning how to recast my sentences along simpler, more direct lines. You can do this too, as a spiritual exercise to avoid making more karma.

But such modifications as better word selection are really cosmetic changes. Daily karma is resolved best through this one simple change: Say and do everything in the name of the SUGMAD, the ECK, or the Mahanta. Then your life will begin to turn around for good.

38. Listening to the Mockingbird

When you go to bed, listen in a gentle, calm way to the night sounds. Sometimes you'll hear the night birds, the hum of air conditioning, the traffic outside, a helicopter flying overhead, or the soft rumble of voices. Just lie in bed and listen. You hear these different sounds so often that you unconsciously erase them from your mind. Put some attention on them now.

While you listen to these physical sounds, sing HU, and then listen for the sacred sounds of ECK. They come in many forms, sometimes as the ringing or tinkling of bells or the sound of musical instruments.

Try to identify as many different physical sounds as you can. Go to sleep with these sounds in your consciousness, all the while knowing they are part of the HU, the universal Sound which embodies all others.

Listen carefully, because in these sounds you will find the secret name of God.

39. Training the Imagination

The imaginative faculty within yourself is like a muscle. You're going to have to train it day after day. What you are actually doing is learning how to become aware and observant of yourself in a different state of consciousness.

One way is to go to different places in your imagination. Maybe you'll want to re-create a plane ride: I'm sitting in the airplane seat. What do I see? What do the people look like? What happens when I walk down the aisle? What is on the food tray?

As you go through the day, you'll find yourself looking at objects and making mental notes, because that physical information about the dresser or the clothes in your closet will be helpful when you sit down in your chair and try to visualize it for Soul Travel.

40. Conquering Fear

The ECK, Divine Spirit, pushes us into a situation where—by agreement, by saying we would like the next-higher stage of illumination—we open ourselves to changes in our life.

The moment we say to the Mahanta, "I am ready; take me where you will," is like the flash of lightning. In the space of time that follows, we face the unknown. We go about our life, changes start to occur, and we don't quite understand what's happening or how it's going to turn out.

If you are afraid of something and feel like you are frozen on the edge of a cliff, close your eyes and imagine the Mahanta reaching out his hand. Visualize him guiding you past the steep ledge to where the path widens into a meadow.

Then Wah Z says, "When you get to areas of the path that are unfamiliar to you, you can use a technique to help you adjust. Begin by singing HU. After a few minutes, you will feel less afraid. Then walk in a small circle once. Sing HU while you walk. This will get you used to this new area."

He shows you how to do it, and you copy him. Then he says, "Each time you walk around, make your circle a little wider. Soon you will be comfortable in the new area."

41. Another Way to Use Your Secret Word

For some ECK initiates, using your secret word when you first have an initiation will bring many grand and glorious experiences. For others it won't. This word opens you only to a room.

But as you get established on the plane of your initiation, you can begin chanting another word, perhaps one for the Mental Plane, or one of the words you find in the *ECKANKAR Dictionary*. It's a password that will get you through one of the doors.

Start by chanting your secret word or the ECK word of a plane, then add another word in conjunction with it. For instance, if you want to look at a past life, add the word for the Causal Plane.

Work at this: Try it out for a week or two. If it doesn't work, then try some other word. Keep trying, but in a gentle way. Don't force it. Assume the attitude that someday you know this is going to work—and you just keep trying.

One day on your inner travels, you'll get to a door leading to another plane. The guardian of the door will say, "Yes?" Then you'll say this word to him, and he'll let you into the hallway. From there you'll enter into another room—a whole new, spiritual dimension.

This is just one more way to use your secret word.

42. Contemplation Seed for Times of Distress

Here is a short contemplation seed the ECK Master Lai Tsi found in himself upon returning from the heavenly worlds. Should anyone be in distress or need to reach the great SUGMAD, use this contemplation. Repeat it slowly. It certainly brings results.

Show me Thy ways, O SUGMAD;
Teach me Thy path.
Lead me in Thy truth, and teach me;
On Thee do I wait all day.
Remember, O Beloved, Thy guiding light
And Thy loving care.
For it has been ever Thy will
To lead the least of Thy servants to Thee!

43. Unruly Thoughts

Unruly thoughts are the enemy of the individual practicing the Spiritual Exercises of ECK. In contemplation, as the mind responds to different stimuli, thoughts crop up continuously.

Watch these thoughts as they arise. Soon you will be aware of thoughts following so closely one upon another that they resemble a river. Gaze unperturbed at the interminable flow of thoughts as if you were sitting on a riverbank watching the water flow past.

Do not try to stop any thought process at this stage, just rise above it. The effort to stop a thought from arising inevitably creates other thoughts. Leave unshaped any concept or idea which appears; become indifferent to these thoughts, neither trying to stop them nor fall under their influence. Work from the Atma Plane, the Soul region, unconcerned with what the mind has to say or how it acts.

Imagine the mind is like a small child looking with interest at a toy. The mind is nothing more than a small child which sometimes becomes unruly and wants attention. Handle the mind as you would a small child.

This stage is called the first resting place. If you are successful to this point, you will have attained freedom from the mental tyranny of thoughts and be ready for greater spiritual tasks.

44. Bathing in Light

If you have a problem or desire a healing, try this exercise before falling asleep.

Catch yourself at that point just before you fall asleep—between waking and sleep. Imagine bathing yourself with healing orange light.

You then can ask the Inner Master to help you regain spiritual balance by saying, "If it's for the good of all concerned and doesn't interfere with my spiritual growth, would you please heal me?" Then holding that thought, drift into a sound sleep.

45. What Is HU?

Singing HU or chanting your secret word enhances your life and gives you strength. HU is a holy name for God which will lift you into the higher worlds.

But the name itself has even more meaning behind it. I would like to recommend a spiritual exercise which will be very beneficial to you in finding it out for yourself.

As you chant each long, drawn-out HU outwardly, keep asking inwardly, "What is HU?" Repeat the question mentally as many times as is comfortable for you, maybe two or three. In other words, with each outward HU, you are asking within, "What is HU? What is HU? What is HU?"

46. Regaining Emotional Balance

If you are faced with negative attitudes about people, how can you feel the love of the Mahanta? Here are three ways:

1. If you meet someone that you have negative feelings about, silently say to yourself, "In the name of the SUGMAD." Repeat this phrase to yourself each time this occurs, blessing the situation and letting it go.

2. Be polite when these people are near you, but chant HU silently within yourself. Listen to them while you chant, rather than getting into a long conversation with them. Say as little as possible while still remaining cordial.

3. In your imagination, see the Mahanta near you.

When you bless a situation, you keep yourself in balance and do not become involved in the negative conditions. In addition, if you are a true channel for the ECK, miracles will take place around you.

47. Bypassing the Mind

This spiritual exercise can help you bypass the mind, which tends to get stuck in a routine. If you have done a spiritual exercise enough times that it becomes a routine, the mind says, I know this path—and immediately runs ahead and puts up blocks.

So you trick the mind by coming at the spiritual exercise from different angles. The mind is reactive, but Soul is active and without limits. You can come up with more creative exercises than the mind can find blocks for.

For a month, alternate the following spiritual exercise with your regular one. You can do this exercise one night, use your regular spiritual exercise the second night, then try this one again the third night.

Imagine walking with the Master on the inner planes. Begin chanting a word which is similar to HU: HUUUACH (HU-ach). It begins with a rough *H,* as is used in the German or Greek languages, then forms into a soft, drawn-out HUU-ach.

All ECK words, or names for God on the different planes, are derivatives of HU. The word given during an ECK initiation is a name for God from a specific plane, tailored to your particular vibration. These names are given for your spiritual upliftment and can be used for your Soul Travel adventures and journeys.

48. Potholes

During the day, each time you find yourself criticizing someone else about anything, stop. Look at yourself very gently, without criticism. Ask, "Is it possible that I am the person I have been criticizing?"

Sing, or chant, the word *ECK*, which purges from the mind the dross of ignorance.

Maybe you thought you were criticizing your friend, but you are really criticizing yourself.

When you realize this, you can take a lot of the potholes out of the road back to God.

To get around barriers on the road to God, an individual must find the Sound and Light, the most certain way to spiritual freedom. A simple contemplative exercise to help one do that is to sing HU.

Chapter Five

Solving Problems

49. Bypassing Barriers

To get around barriers on the road to God, an individual must find the Sound and Light, the most certain way to spiritual freedom. A simple contemplative exercise to help one do that is this: At bedtime, shut your eyes and look at a blank screen in your mind. This screen is located at the Spiritual Eye, which is slightly above and behind the eyebrows. Breathe deeply several times, then sing *God* or *HU* softly for twenty minutes.

To add variety to your contemplations, look at the letters *E-C-K,* which signify the Holy Spirit. Whatever name you choose, sing it daily. This word may be sung aloud—or silently, if you do not want to disturb another. It is often enough to mentally invite the Mahanta, the Living ECK Master to give you a Soul Travel experience during sleep. No harm will come to you, for a Soul Traveler of the Far Country is always there to watch over you.

Before contemplation, think of some person you love, or of some happy event. This feeling of love or goodwill is necessary for travel in the Far Country. Soul Travel is the first step to God.

50. Creative Process

To solve problems, work with the creative cycle in ECK. When you come up against something, try to put it into a question.

On the other planes, sometimes the Mahanta, the Living ECK Master sits at a table with the rest of the ECK Masters, and they talk things out. According to the way we regard ECK Masters, any one of them ought to be smart enough to handle anything that goes on. So why do they talk things out?

This is simply an educational process. We learn what a Master does and how he works with the ECK, or Divine Spirit. How do you work with the ECK? It's easy to say, "Just let the ECK take care of it," then sit back and wait. But that is not always going to work. A better way is as follows.

First, figure out what's wrong and say, "Something's going wrong. This is the title I've given to what's going wrong. Now I would like an answer for how it can go right."

Next, contemplate on the problem and look at it from every angle. You may talk it over with everybody who's got the least bit of knowledge about it. Eventually, if you ask a good question, the answer is going to suggest itself. At some point, it's going to become very clear what to do.

51. The Stone Statue

Before you go to sleep, imagine seeing yourself as a statue. Visualize the ECK Masters Peddar Zaskq, Rebazar Tarzs, Fubbi Quantz, and Wah Z gathered around the statue with moving equipment. Wah Z and Peddar Zaskq each have a crowbar, while Fubbi Quantz and Rebazar Tarzs are operating a tow truck.

Visualize Peddar and Wah Z prying up the edge of the statue and the hoist from the tow truck being slipped under it. The tow truck groans under the dead weight of the statue, but it lifts it. How high it lifts it doesn't matter.

The Masters now move the statue from one place to another—from the Physical to the Astral to the Causal Plane. Fubbi Quantz then drives the tow truck up a ramp into a Temple of Golden Wisdom where they have a restoration room. In this big, empty room the ECK Masters turn statues back into living spiritual beings.

The ECK Masters are all very happy that they have gotten the statue this far. It's a lateral move but better than no move at all. Fubbi Quantz carefully lowers the statue and sets it down in the center of the room. He brings in a few plants, including large ferns, and places them around the statue to make it pretty.

Now watch carefully to see what the ECK Masters are doing.

Each Master has a little can, which he pries open with a screwdriver. Inside is a very special oil designed to dissolve crust, the crust of ages, the kind of crust that gets on Soul after being hardened by the problems of daily living.

The ECK Masters very carefully put this dissolving oil all over the statue. Remember the statue is you. Shift your viewpoint from watching what is happening, to being the statue itself. Feel the dissolving oil being smeared all over you. After a moment, the crust of ages begins to crumble, and underneath it is healthy skin.

The ECK Masters stand back and look. "There's somebody in there," they cry jokingly. They watch as Soul breaks free of the human consciousness. When this happens, the ceiling opens up and the sun, or Light of God, touches the real being that was trapped inside the statue of human consciousness.

Repeat this exercise for one month. As you progress in the Light and Sound, the ECK will begin to enliven your spiritual pulse. You will begin to listen, and you will hear the Sound of the spheres, which may sound like the wind in the trees.

52. Law of Reversed Effort

If you feel you are trying too hard to accomplish something, consider the Law of Reversed Effort. This law is a practical law of nature concerned with the use of the imaginative powers.

It goes like this: The more you concentrate on putting your imaginative powers upon something, the less you are able to do it. Or, the harder one struggles to avoid something the more it will be attracted to him.

For example, when one is trying to ride a bicycle and avoid hitting any rocks on the road, he is so conscious of hitting the rocks he'll probably do so. Or if a person tries to walk across a small plank from one building to another at the tenth floor, his mind would be on falling, not on walking.

This law is concerned with imagining and feeling. The negative thoughts are apt to be more effective than the positive, because the negative usually has more feeling with it.

Take your goal into contemplation and focus on relaxing, letting go the negative feelings associated with not achieving this goal. Set up a positive image about the goal, then put feeling with it. It's that simple.

53. Viewing Difficulties

This exercise allows you to see why long-lasting or hard-to-solve problems are still with you.

In contemplation, look at your problem and ask yourself which of these viewpoints you hold about it.

1. You view the problem as a battering ram. When it approaches, you fall over backward, flattened to the ground.
2. You view the problem as a vital, valuable lesson which will teach you something. You believe it will become a spiritual springboard to give you the necessary incentive and energy to climb up and out of your present situation.

Your attitude about your problem holds the key to whether your experience with it will be easy or difficult, long or short.

Those people who have spiritual success don't say, "Oh, no!" and fall down when a problem comes up. They look to see the reason or lesson behind it. They ask the Mahanta, "What can I learn from it? How has it made me stronger?"

54. Game of Chess

You can do this exercise anytime—whether you are at work, in contemplation, or about to fall asleep.

Lightly place your attention upon a situation in your life, then put your viewpoint as Soul above the situation. Look down on everything going on below as if it were a chess game—even though it might be in your imagination. You can look at a situation anywhere in the world from this viewpoint.

As you are gazing upon it, change the situation by simply rearranging your place on the chessboard. It's a successful device, and those who use it often make great changes around themselves.

55. Sherlock Holmes Technique

If there is a problem that you can't seem to work through, you may wish to try the following exercise.

Shut your eyes, and begin to visualize Sherlock Holmes in his funny-looking cap. First, you see a luminous blue form, which then begins to look like Sherlock Holmes holding a magnifying glass in front of him. He's walking along a path toward you. As he gets closer, you see that he is the Mahanta, the Living ECK Master.

The Mahanta greets you, then says, "If you'll come with me, we'll go find a solution to your problem."

As you begin to follow the Mahanta, the Inner Master in the guise of Sherlock Holmes, you become more and more aware of the incredibly bright blue light around him. You become more aware also that the light passes through his magnifying glass like a flashlight. Together you walk through a misty marsh, and the Blue Light of ECK illuminates the path.

As you go with him, you may chant the word *HUUUACH* (HU-ach). It's similar to HU. You can use this word with this particular exercise as you are walking along with the Inner Master, who will be dressed like Sherlock Holmes.

Finally, you come to an enormous rock. The Mahanta, still dressed as Sherlock, easily lifts it. He holds his magnifying glass up for you to see. The blue light shining through the glass has turned to white light. And on the bottom of the rock, you see engraved the solution to your problem.

Do this exercise every other night for one month, interchanging it with your regular spiritual exercise. It's an attempt to bypass the mind. See what you discover.

56. The Shariyat Technique

The following technique is a down-to-earth exercise that is geared to finding the Light and Sound of God. Many who have had difficulty with the imaginative techniques for Soul Travel will find this method successful.

1. Form a question about a problem that has been bothering you in your life. The question can be about health, prosperity, love, or any other subject that has been troubling you.

2. Open *The Shariyat-Ki-Sugmad,* Book One or Two, at random. Read one paragraph and then close your eyes. Sing, or chant, HU eight times (eight corresponds to the eight outer initiations) and then contemplate the passage you have just read. Continue this quiet contemplation for about five minutes, then chant HU eight more times. Again, return to quiet contemplation on the paragraph from *The Shariyat.* Follow this procedure a third time. The entire contemplation will take from fifteen to twenty minutes.

3. Open *The Shariyat* at random again and read another paragraph. See how this paragraph relates to the first paragraph, how both offer a new insight and approach to your problem.

The usual reason a problem exists for us is that we are afraid to take the next step. Often we can think of four or five solutions to a problem, but we argue with ourselves, trying to decide what the next step should be.

The Shariyat may tell you what the next step is. You may wish to go through the technique again on the following day to carry the solution one step further or to explore some new question of a spiritual nature.

57. A Technique to Go Slower

Life puts you in situations that can cause you to panic. You have to remember to calm down, to get yourself, Soul, back in control of the mind. That helps you think clearly enough to see what needs to be done. Then you can take care of the situation.

Patience and composure are among the attributes of an ECK chela. What can you do to develop these two qualities in yourself?

In contemplation ask the Inner Master what you can do to go slower. Once you've figured out this secret, you can be patient. You can let the storms of life blow over you while you think of a way to find shelter.

One way is through surrender. Tonight, before you go to sleep, speak to the Mahanta. Say, "I am a child of thine. Take me where you will, to show me the ways of SUGMAD."

Soul—the spiritual principle, the creative spark of God—cannot work if you panic. Anxiety shuts down the creative centers. When you can't think, whatever you try to do becomes one blunder piled upon another. If you slow down, the spiritual principle can begin working through you so that you can figure out the solution to the problem that is bothering you.

58. The Purifying Sound

Close your eyes and look to the Spiritual Eye. Sing HU, an old and secret name for God. It is one of the most powerful words for spiritual upliftment that I can give you.

As you sing HU, listen for the Sound. The Sound may be heard in any number of different ways. It can be like a train going by, a bird, buzzing bees, sometimes a flute, or even guitars. The way you hear It just depends on where you are.

These sounds are the action of the Holy Spirit, the ECK, as Its atoms vibrate in the invisible worlds. The Sound you hear is the vibration at the particular level to which you are attuned at the time.

Imagine the Sound purifying you, removing the impurities of Soul. It will bring you an understanding of how your actions have caused your problems. It will also give you an indication of what you can do to unfold and how to figure out the way to do things right.

59. Opening the Heart Center

Many people want to know how to get rid of fear. Fear isn't something you can be talked out of. The secret to getting rid of fear is to open the heart center.

In contemplation, imagine yourself sitting in the audience at an ECKANKAR seminar, with the Living ECK Master speaking from the stage. Visualize the golden Light of God coming into your heart center, coming in so quietly and gently that you may not realize It's there. Imagine your heart center reacting like the pupil of an eye, opening gently to allow more Light to come in.

There is a way for each person to control the opening of the heart center and the flow of Light within. Ask the Inner Master how to maintain the inner connection with the ECK to find a balance that is right for you.

60. The Master's Presence

As you sit in contemplation, ask the Inner Master for more understanding of the words *I am always with you.*

Practice talking inwardly to the Master about anything that is in your heart. Visualize him sitting right next to you and establish a dialogue. One day you may be surprised to hear him answer you, loud and clear.

Practice of the Master's presence is one of the four fundamentals of ECK.

You are preparing to enter the inner temple, that sacred place where Soul has communication with God.

Chapter Six

The Light and Sound of God

61. The Temple Door

This is a very simple exercise to make contact with the Voice of God.

Close your eyes and relax. You are preparing to enter the inner temple, that sacred place where Soul has communication with God. You may see the Light of God first in your Spiritual Eye. You may see It as a Blue Light or a Blue Star. You may see It as a globe or blob of light.

This means you have contact with the highest state of consciousness that is available. It can uplift you to that very same state, too, but not overnight—the shock would be too great.

After you see the Light in your Spiritual Eye or feel It in your heart center, then comes the Sound. The Sound may come first at times.

The Sound may be that of the flute of God which comes from the Soul Plane. Or you may hear the buzzing of bees or any number of different sounds. Later, as you move higher, it may become a very high peeping sound, a single peep so high that it feels as if you can barely reach it.

It is the Voice of God uplifting you.

62. Golden Musical Notes

Sit or lie down, close your eyes, and place your attention on the Spiritual Eye. Chant HU. As you chant, listen carefully in a gentle way. Use the creative imagination: Try to visualize the Sound as golden musical notes flowing down from a place above you.

As you see them, know that each golden note has an accompanying sound. Listen for the melodies as they pass into and through you in a continuous stream.

Visualize something connected with the music that strikes a definite image on your mind, perhaps a stringed instrument, a flute, or woodwinds. First try to see, then try to hear the golden notes flowing down from this musical instrument. Know that you are listening to the melody of God.

63. On the Rooftops

Imagine yourself placing a ladder against the house. Anchor it very securely with ropes, then climb the ladder and sit on the rooftop, staying within reach of the ladder.

Listen for a rushing wind. This is how the ECK, or Holy Spirit, sounds at a certain level when you are listening with the spiritual ears of Soul. Sometimes It comes as a high-energy sound, as though you were standing next to a jet engine, a huge motor, or a dynamo. If you hear It for even a brief time, this is good. It means that the action of the ECK is working in you, purifying and uplifting.

If you're afraid the wind might blow you off the roof, look at it another way: The ECK will blow you into new circumstances in your outer life. As above, so below.

When the sound of the Holy Spirit begins to come through Soul, to purify and cleanse, you can remember the ladder. It's nearby if you need it. Feel secure that you won't be blown off into the dark unknown.

And when the fear subsides, you'll be led into the next step very naturally.

64. The Mountain of God

Find a quiet place where no one will disturb you for ten or fifteen minutes. Then shut your eyes and look at a place just above and between the eyebrows. That is the location of the Spiritual Eye.

Now imagine you are climbing to the top of a broad green mountain. Follow the brown dirt path to a meadow of colorful flowers. Powder white clouds near the summit of the mountain give a feeling of great joy, wonder, and freedom. This is the Mountain of God.

When you reach the top, lie down upon the thick, soft carpet of grass. Feel the sunshine warm your face, arms, and body. Shut your eyes there, too, as you did when you began this exercise in your room. For the moment, expect complete darkness of the inner vision.

Now look gently for the Light of God to appear in your Spiritual Eye. It may appear in a number of ways. It may come as a soft field of light, similar to the fluffy white clouds near the mountaintop. Again, It may be a pinpoint of light: blue, white, yellow, purple, or even green or pink.

While looking for the Light, softly sing HU over and over again. It is Soul's love song to God. Without staring, continue to watch for the Light within your Spiritual Eye. Listen also for the Sound.

The Sound of God is the vibration of Divine Spirit moving the atoms of life. You may hear the sound of a flute, a rushing wind, the chirping of birds, a waterfall, bells, or the buzzing of bees. These are actual, not imaginary, sounds.

Return to the Mountain of God for a few minutes every day. That journey in contemplation is one of the surest ways to find divine love.

65. The Surat Technique

Sit comfortably. Put both hands in your lap, fingers interlaced with palms up, then place your attention on the Tisra Til, the Spiritual Eye.

Take five deep breaths and begin chanting the word *HU,* the universal name of God. For this exercise, chant it in two syllables, as H-U, and sing it in a long, drawn-out manner. After some time has elapsed, take five more deep breaths and continue softly chanting HU. Keep your attention fixed on the Tisra Til. Don't try to see anything, just hold it there.

After a while, again repeat the five deep breaths, bringing the total to fifteen. Following this, slow down your chanting until it is very, very slow. Begin to listen to what you are singing. Chant slower still, until you stop completely. Switch your attention to listening to the esoteric sounds as the word *HU* rolls through you. It starts vibrating like a machine. You may even shake, but don't let this frighten you.

Very soon you'll begin to hear a humming sound in the back of your head, spreading out to your body, until you become part of the sound. Then various parts of the ECK melody will start. Sometimes it is the roaring of a waterfall. Other times it is the sound of violins or flutes.

This means you are somewhere on the far planes of the higher worlds, beyond the Fifth, or Soul, Plane, traveling in the Soul body in the realms of God.

66. Movie Screen

Find a comfortable position and relax. Shut your eyes, and look at the inner screen. Imagine you are watching a movie screen. Sometimes it will be black, sometimes white, sometimes gray. There may even be times when you can see a scene or a moving picture.

At first, try looking straight at the screen. After a while this may not work, so let your inner vision stray to the left or right about ten degrees. Suddenly, out of the corner of your eye, you may notice that something has appeared on the screen. This is how you begin to look for the Master.

In a relaxed way, look obliquely, knowing that your attention is really to the center. Begin singing HU or chanting your secret word.

As you do this spiritual exercise and sing HU to yourself, it begins a purifying, cleansing action on Soul. Old habit patterns—the gossip, the idle chatter, the dishonesty with oneself—start to fall away.

67. The Nirat Technique

In using this technique, you will find the path to the other worlds illuminated by Soul's own light, much like the headlights of a car, cutting through the darkness of night, illuminate the road ahead. The Nirat technique utilizes the seeing power of Soul.

Sit in silence, with the attention fixed on the Spiritual Eye. Put your attention on the Light of God, the white light within the door of the Spiritual Eye. This is the subtle gateway to the Astral world, the first door you will pass through on the way to higher worlds.

With your attention fixed on this door, look obliquely—not directly—at whatever appears on the screen of the mind. If you look at it directly, it will disappear. But if you look at it from an angle, the image of the light will stay.

Now very softly begin to practice the zikar, the repetition of the holy names of God. If you are an initiate, use your secret word. If you are not, sing the word for each plane that you must pass through in order to reach the Soul region. These are: *Alayi* (Physical Plane), *Kala* (Astral Plane), *Mana* (Causal Plane), *Aum* (Mental Plane), *Baju* (Etheric Plane), and *SUGMAD* (Soul Plane). By these sounds you are able to lift yourself up through the corresponding planes into the Soul world.

The Light of God appears on all planes, but the light that should interest you most is the Blue Star. It will come into focus after the technique has been practiced for a certain length of time. This star represents the Mahanta, the Living ECK Master, who will later appear in his radiant body.

Sometimes the Master appears as a Blue Star, sometimes as a misty, pale blue light. The star or light will lead you gently through the various planes into the Soul region. You must trust It completely, never being doubtful or hesitant about following It, nor wondering where It may lead you.

As Soul gets collected and concentrates on the Spiritual Eye, you will have some preliminary experiences of the inner sounds and sights. These occur before Soul is settled down and actually traveling in the inner worlds. You may hear sounds similar to a moving train, whistles, or stringed instruments. Then you will hear sounds like the tinkling of small bells, progressing to the ringing notes of a large bell. Following this are lights similar to the glowing of charcoal, then lightning, and finally the gigantic star.

Then you are able to see a whole starry sky. You see the Lightning and Moon worlds, and you are ready for the ascent. You may see forms as mist, smoke, suns, fire, winds, fireflies, lightning, crystals, and moons. Your attention may be scattered at this point, but bring it back and focus again on a single point.

68. A Way to Fill Yourself with Love

If you wish to approach God, you must first be filled with love. If you are filled with fear, frustration, or any of the lower negative states, you will have nothing but failure.

One way to fill yourself with love is by recalling the image of something from the past that brought great happiness to you.

Read a passage from *Stranger by the River* to open your heart. Then in contemplation, ask yourself, "Where is the key to love?" Imagine something or someone you love. Use this as a conductor of love.

As Soul, place yourself above the Time Track. Notice all of the truly happy moments from your life. Visualize the happiness as waves rolling upon a beach. Then collect some of it, and going forward on the Time Track, sprinkle the living waters of this happiness throughout your present and future.

Leave it there to bring forth the gifts of Divine Spirit later. Now slowly return to the physical with the knowledge that happiness and love await you both in the present and in the years to come.

If we want to keep the blessings of life coming to us, we must learn to be grateful for what we have and for whatever is given. This gratitude begins to create a series of events for our spiritual benefit.

69. A Wonderland of Love

Do this technique at bedtime. Shut your eyes as you prepare to go to sleep. Far off in the distance, look for a dot of golden light. It will be dim at first, then it will grow in size and intensity as it moves rapidly toward you.

Watch it grow in size until you see it is the ᘓ symbol—the letters EK. Its color is that of an old bronze metal with a good many dents on the polished surface. This demonstrates the enduring nature of ECK.

Concentrate upon the golden letters ᘓ, and softly chant HU, the sacred name of God. Soon you should see the Light and hear the Sound of God. This is your key to the wonderland of God's divine love.

70. SUGMAD's Music

Chant the letters of the word *SUGMAD,* which means God, going up a musical scale. Sing the letter *S* as the deep bass note, and raise the pitch as you sing each succeeding letter: *S-U-G-M-A-D.* End with *D* on the highest possible note.

Then start over again, beginning with the lowest note and going up the musical scale. Continue this exercise for twenty minutes, unless you feel strain on your vocal chords.

In the weeks that follow, watch your life for positive changes. The ECK pushes us into a situation where, by agreement that we would like the next higher stage of illumination, we open ourselves to changes in this life.

71. The Water of Life

In contemplation or before going to sleep, visualize yourself walking along a beach.

Ahead of you on the sand is a blanket spread with fruit. The Inner Master, the Mahanta, is waiting for you. In his hands he holds a goblet made of precious jewels.

The Mahanta offers you the goblet. "This is the water of life," he says to you. "Take it, and drink."

The water of life is actually the ECK, which is the Light and Sound of God. As you drink of It, visualize the Light and Sound rushing through your being. Know that once you drink of this, you will never be the same. You will always thirst for the waters of heaven.

72. Meeting the Master

Take a comfortable sitting position on your bed or in a chair. Gaze gently and sweetly into the Spiritual Eye between the eyebrows.

Everything may appear dark for a moment. Gaze into the space between the brows minutely and more minutely. Look for the Light, a sheet of white light.

The Light may be like a great sun, throwing Its glittering, brilliant rays in a circle around you. Its brilliancy greater than ten thousand suns.

Suddenly you realize that the Light is coming from within yourself, spreading into an ever-widening circle until It fills the whole universe. It flows out of a center within you and becomes a burning beacon. Feel your whole body pulse with the rhythm of Its surging waves like the pounding of surf upon a sandy beach.

You hear the roaring of the surf in your ears, and it grows and grows. Suddenly into your inner vision steps the Mahanta, the Living ECK Master. Greet him with joy in your heart and begin your journey into the worlds of God.

This is one of the steps to self-mastery: learning how to have the discipline to very directly face what's causing you trouble.

Chapter Seven

Self-Discipline

73. Write It Down

So often people who fail say, "I simply cannot deal with my life. Everything is wrong. I can't get over this problem."

When you're feeling very upset and down on the world, when you feel at odds with people, when you don't have the confidence you want, sit down and write an initiate report.

In the first paragraph or two, write what's bothering you. Try to do this in the first or second sentence if you can condense it that much. Say, "This is what's troubling me. I can't handle it." Then keep writing the details. Put in some of the experiences that have happened that support the situation.

You might write, "I'm having this problem with somebody at work, and here are some of the things this person has done to me."

As you're writing the details, after about five, ten, or fifteen minutes, you're going to find something is lifting from you. The problem won't be as heavy as it was before.

If those feelings come back again in a day or a week or a month, sit down again and write. This is your self-discipline. This is one of the steps to self-mastery: learning how to have the discipline to very directly face what's causing you trouble.

Everyone comes into this life with a debt.

In some situations, there's a karmic cause that goes way back. Some things you have to live with, like poor eyesight. But other things you don't have to live with.

When you're working with the Mahanta, he can go back beyond birth. If you give these problems over to the Mahanta in an initiate report, in your dream state he can begin unwinding the past karma. No one else can do that for you.

74. Radio Announcer

If there are missing pieces of information regarding some aspect of your life—for example, a disturbing dream or a problem—try this technique to help fill in the blanks.

Go into contemplation, and listen for the Sound of ECK. Visualize turning on a radio. Next, imagine the radio announcer coming on. Listen as he summarizes the details of a dream or problem whose meaning is unclear.

Now sing HU for a few minutes to relax. This is like taking a commercial break. Then imagine the radio announcer saying, "And now, here's the rest of your dream." Imagine the narrator filling in the missing pieces of the dream and unraveling its meaning.

When you have a bad dream, the dream censor has not allowed the whole story to come out. Begin with the assumption that something's missing, that you don't know everything yet. Then use the inner faculties to get the answers you need.

75. The Dream Basket

In contemplation or the dream state, imagine meeting the Inner Master in your home or office. He holds out a wastebasket. "Take your cares and worries, and put them in here," he tells you.

Visualize taking all the things that are bothering you and putting them into the Master's basket. Feel rested and relaxed as you release them into the hands of the ECK.

If something is unpleasant in your life, change it. You are the creator of your worlds, whether they are on the inner planes or out here. The Inner Master will try to show you how to make your life out here better.

By turning a situation over to the Inner Master, something is worked off, and out of it can come more harmony and balance.

76. Monkeys of the Mind

You can work with the imagination not only on the inner planes but out here too. For instance, if you see a dog coming down the street who looks as if he would like to bite you, visualize a loving situation. Keep your attention on loving the dog—petting him, playing with him, and scratching him behind his ears. It's a good spiritual exercise, and it may also keep his teeth marks off you. Of course, it never hurts to give him a wide berth too.

The same principle can be used on the inner planes when your mind jumps around. You can visualize your thoughts as monkeys jumping around and see what you can do to make them calm down instead of being mischievous. You're working with an imaginative technique here, which gives you a multitude of possibilities.

Visualize a door that you want to walk through, but you can't because the monkeys are jumping all around in front of it. Say to yourself, I've got to get the monkeys quieted down, and then I can go through the door and enter into the worlds of Light and Sound.

Give the monkeys bright, attractive little toys with bells, or feed them bananas. You can get so involved in quieting the monkeys of the mind that you'll find you're enjoying yourself. Soul is now expressing Itself.

As soon as you get them settled down, make a dash for the door. On the other side is the pure golden Light of God. Know that the Master is there. He's saying to you, "I'm here whenever you can get past the monkeys."

The monkeys of the mind are merely the guardians of the door. They'll do everything possible to keep you from going through. Once you figure out a way to calm them down, then you're ready to go beyond into the inner worlds.

77. Stepping-Stones

Some people never recognize the blessings they receive. Others may look back and realize they've had a gift of healing of some sort. Maybe something has changed at work to make their life better. But it depends upon the individual— how conscious you are.

A spiritual exercise to begin recognizing your gifts is this: Sing HU quietly to yourself or out loud. Look at the obstacles in your life that you think are stumbling blocks. Imagine them becoming stepping-stones. How are they teaching you about yourself? Open yourself and gain greater awareness of this as you sing HU.

The teachings of ECK are all about God's love for you. HU is an ancient name for God that is the key to your secret worlds. Once you learn to use this key, you will find a blending of your inner and outer worlds. You'll find yourself filling with love.

78. Discussing Inner Experiences

If you're curious about which spiritual experiences should not be discussed, try this technique. The way of ECK is one of experience, so use the trial-and-error method to see which inner experiences are too sacred for public discussion.

Keep track of your inner experiences for a given period of time and talk of them to your usual confidants. Be aware of what happens.

If you are speaking of things which are for you alone, you will soon know. What happens is that the Mahanta begins to shut down the individual's memory of the secret teachings that are given to him. Within a month or two you will become aware that the golden hand of the Mahanta's love and protection has been withdrawn. You will feel empty and alone.

When you are convinced of the emptiness that comes of giving the secret teachings of the Mahanta to those who have no right to them, then make it a practice to keep all the inner happenings to yourself. It will take one or two months before the channel to the ECK will open you to the secret teachings again.

This experiment can be done as often as proof is needed that the secret instructions of the Mahanta are for you alone. Finally, one's self-discipline becomes such that he tells no one but the Master anything, because the penalty of living without the love and protection of the Mahanta is not worth the trouble.

79. A Little Box of ECK

To help you counteract negative thoughts during moments of crisis, try this idea suggested by an ECK youth. Make an "ECK box." Cut out about twenty-four small pieces of paper; on each paper write a different ECK principle, loving thought, or lighthearted idea.

Some examples are:

"Soul doesn't have a shadow."

"I love you."

"Let the Master guide you."

"Don't let the Kal, the negative power, interfere with your life."

Whenever you feel mad or sad, pull out a piece of paper and read it aloud.

These small reminders from the ECK will help chase negative thoughts away. They can lighten up the darker attitudes that slip into our consciousness now and then.

80. Four Disciplines of ECK

During your day, practice these spiritual disciplines.

1. **Cleanliness of mind.** Let no words which would pollute the air enter into your mind. Look upon everyone as creatures of God, for they, like yourself, are temples who shall eventually become Co-workers with God. Fast continuously from all Kal (negative) thoughts which could infect your mental state and consciousness. Through this you learn the powerful awareness of the presence of the Living ECK Master, who is with you constantly.

2. **Patience.** This is the greatest discipline of all the spiritual works of ECK. By patience you can endure life, hardships, karmic burdens, slander, and the pricks of pain and disease. Keep your mind steadfastly upon the Light of God, never swerving, never letting up on your attention to the goal of God-Realization.

3. **Humility and chastity.** As you come to know these attributes in your life, you learn all your responsibility belongs to God, not to anyone nor anything within this physical realm. Your loved ones, family, and relatives are images of God, mirrored in this worldly life and embodiment to serve the SUGMAD,

the Supreme Deity. Realize that humility is opposite to the ego. Do not let a false concept of your worth to the Master and to the SUGMAD stand in your way to reach the heavenly states. Know that vanity is only a trap of the negative power, Kal Niranjan, and you will become a fool if you let yourself be enslaved by Kal.

4. **Discrimination.** Learn to discriminate between all things, that there is no good nor evil, no beauty nor ugliness, and no sin. These are all concepts of the mind, the dual forces in the matter worlds. Once you recognize and understand this, you will then be free of Kal traps. You will be ready to enter into the Kingdom of God, the Ocean of Love and Mercy. You will be the ECK, of Itself.

To work with an open heart is to love or care for something or someone more than you do for yourself. This is the first step to the divine love we are looking for.

Chapter Eight

Open-Eyed Techniques

81. The Open Heart

In this spiritual exercise, you practice keeping an open heart throughout everyday life. It's very tough; I have to work at it all the time too.

No one technique will work for everyone, but there are ways to keep your attention on having an open heart. Start with something you can love, even a pet or a plant, and just love it a lot. As the love comes, let it pour through you.

The habit of love is catching; it builds, gains momentum, and becomes easier. But like a plant that needs watering and loving care every day, the habit of love takes constant attention.

Love won't come through unless the heart is open. To work with an open heart is to love or care for something or someone more than you do for yourself. This is the first step to the divine love that we are looking for.

82. Two Disciplines

One of the simplest disciplines in ECK is repeating to yourself the name of the Living ECK Master or one of the other ECK Masters. You can set a goal, like repeating the name one thousand times before stopping.

Another discipline is that of reading a portion of *The Shariyat-Ki-Sugmad* each day over a period of several months. Start at the beginning and read straight through without missing a day's study.

Through practice of these disciplines, you'll certainly notice a change in yourself.

83. Fasting

This exercise can be done every Friday. The recommended fast is a mental fast. It means keeping your attention on the Mahanta all day long. There are several ways to do it. One way is to sing HU inwardly or outwardly. Another way is to chant your secret word. Still another is to do everything that day in the name of the Mahanta.

You can keep your attention on the Inner Master as much as you can, or you can consciously remove every negative thought that comes up. Visualize it being put into the ECK Life Stream where the Light and Sound of God can neutralize it. The mental fast is especially good for those who have health concerns and cannot abstain from food. It does not need the approval of a physician, and it is the most convenient for anyone to use for their spiritual growth.

The second kind of fast is a partial fast, where you eat one meal or drink fruit juices and eat fruit.

The third method is to do a twenty-four-hour fast drinking only water, if your health permits.

The path of ECK is the middle path. As such, one need not indulge in excesses of any kind to gain spirituality—and this includes the stress of food fasts. The mental fast is both easy and difficult, much harder than the water or partial fast if done correctly. It means keeping your attention upon the Mahanta all day long on Friday.

A special day of fasting helps you develop the inner discipline to reach God-Realization. You learn the habit of being in ECK. Every moment. Every day. In time you will find it more easy and natural than ever to be in a high state of being every moment of your life.

84. Thinking from the End

Thinking from the end means the ability to visualize your desires and give them life by filling them with feeling. Think of a goal, then set intermediate steps leading to it. You can practice this as a spiritual exercise during the day with any goal you might have.

To reach the state of God-Realization, put yourself in the ECK Master's shoes and each time you confront a problem ask: What would the Mahanta do in this situation? Then do it. That's thinking from the end.

The ECK is continually pressing forward for expression through you. Thinking from the end is the creative process that makes life a controllable and enjoyable thing.

85. Attention Shift

If something is getting you down, here's a technique that never fails to work. It's simply a matter of raising the consciousness, of shifting the attention to the ECK and away from what is bothering you.

All you have to do is this: Stop thinking about the difficulty, whatever it is, and think about the ECK, Divine Spirit, instead. This is the complete rule.

It is really just shifting the attention from one point to another.

86. Sharing HU

When you see the opportunity to share the ECK with someone who needs to know something about life, the most important thing you can give them is the HU. This is the ancient and sacred name of God. You may not need to mention ECKANKAR at all, depending on the situation.

Simply tell the person about the HU. Tell them they can sing it quietly at any time to open themselves to the love of God. This can be a spiritual exercise for you.

As the pace of karma speeds up in today's world, many of the conventional religions are simply not flexible enough to meet the growing spiritual needs of people. By sharing the HU with those we encounter, we can act as divine channels for the ECK. We can help someone find the spiritual assistance they want in their life.

87. Doorway to Heaven

Every time you walk through a doorway today, whether at work or at home, know that on the inner planes you are walking through a doorway to heaven. And that is every doorway, as long as you recognize this in your consciousness.

For example, suppose you have a difficult meeting with your boss or co-workers. As you walk through the door into the meeting, know that you are entering the room with a newer, higher consciousness.

When you get inside the room, pause a moment and ask yourself, How is my higher awareness going to affect me? Will I be more relaxed? More tolerant and patient? Will I trust Divine Spirit to provide me with the answers and guidance I need?

If you experiment with this technique, you will find it changes your viewpoint and lifts you higher and higher in awareness throughout the day.

88. More Than Just Getting By

Pick one day a week where you will do more than just get by. On that day put your whole heart into taking care of your family, your work, and yourself.

So many people spend their lives just trying to get by. That's all they really want to do. A person like that isn't material for God Consciousness; his cloth is different from one who is striving for the highest spiritual states.

People of the Golden Heart care about things. They are filled with love, they finish what they start, and they like to see it done well.

89. Broom Technique

When you feel that the negative powers are preventing you from carrying out something important, you can use this technique to clear your path. For example, say you are on an airplane about to leave for an ECK seminar when a distant storm front causes the air traffic controllers to reroute traffic. The following technique can neutralize the Kal, or negative, force in many situations.

This is a visualization technique. Sit back in your seat and shut your eyes. Inwardly sing HU, the ancient name of God. Then, in your Spiritual Eye, see yourself at two locations: (*a*) in the stranded airplane and (*b*) safely at the airport of your destination.

Next, mock up an image of a long-handled broom. While continuing to chant HU, sweep a clean path in your imagination between points A and B.

Then act "as if" you were lord of your own universe. Through the inner channels, have the air traffic controller clear the flight for takeoff.

Be careful with this exercise because there is a fine line between the spiritual and psychic arts. The difference is this: Never manipulate anyone to fit your projects by invisible energy. If, however, you have entered into an agreement with an organization (such as an airline) and something there sidetracks the carrying out of your arrangement, consider it an intrusion into your psychic space by the Kal power.

Say, for instance, your travel agent gets you a ticket for a flight to another city. Your ticket is paid for, the flight is scheduled, and you are seated on the plane. In the meantime, the negative power generates a storm to stall your plane's departure. This is a valid case in which to try this spiritual exercise.

When not to use it: On the spur of the moment you plan to fly somewhere on vacation. At the airline counter an agent informs you the flight is sold out. Do not try to conjure up the secret forces to induce the ticket agent to find you a seat.

90. Sharpen Your Perceptions

For this exercise you will need a notebook. Look at a picture, or take a walk and look at some scenery. Note every detail you can about what you see: shapes, colors, lines, forms, textures, and so on. Then go to your notebook, and write down as much detail as you can.

You will probably be surprised how little you remember. For example, walk by a house. When you get home, can you remember how many windows it had? What kind of door did it have? Was the roof shakes or tiles? What sort of shrubs were in the yard, and if there was a fence, how was it constructed? Later, go back and compare your notes with the house.

Do this again and again, until you can accurately recall the subject of your interest. A fun way to practice this technique is with a friend. Take a walk together, and choose something to study carefully. Then, on your way home, see what details you can both remember.

For those who wish to have better recall of conversations and experiences from their Soul Travel journeys, try this variation: After a conversation with someone or after listening to a recording of words or music, see how much detail you can recall. These simple techniques, practiced over time, will prove rewarding for remembering your inner journeys.

91. When You Have a Busy Day

When you have a job that doesn't leave time to do the spiritual exercises regularly, or at the same time each day, here is a technique to try.

Chant your secret word or sing HU quietly to yourself. Do this for a while during the day and as you go to sleep at night. If your schedule is such that it doesn't allow time for you to sit up and do the twenty-minute spiritual exercise, you can also do a technique that I have used fairly often myself.

Just before you go to sleep, you can say to the Inner Master: "I give you full permission to take me to the place that I have earned or where I can learn something." Then go to sleep, and don't give it another thought.

The Inner Master will begin working with you in the dream state. Often you will find that as your consciousness changes, your outer circumstances may change too. It may take a couple of years. This is the physical world, and often it's very hard.

But the ECK Masters begin working with us where they find us. In the spiritual works, we begin at the point where we are. We can wish for all the leisure time in the world, but the fact is, we have to really look at where we are and then consider what we are going to do in our own circumstances.

The ECK will take us one step at a time inwardly, and this will reflect outwardly in some way. Your life may not be easier, but it will certainly become more adventuresome.

With the help of the Inner Master, the Mahanta, you are learning to take charge of your life. You are becoming the aware Soul, the creator of your own worlds.

Chapter Nine

Mastering Your Fate

92. Finding a New Word

You're doing the spiritual exercises, using
the word you were given at your initiation. Lo
and behold, two weeks pass and the word doesn't
work anymore. Here you are, out in a remote
area, probably at least a couple hundred miles
from the nearest ECK Initiator. You wonder,
What should I do now? I got a word, but it
doesn't work anymore. Sometimes your word
will last through all the different initiations,
from the Second on up; other times it will last
for two initiations and then you need a new one.
So what do you do?

Begin working to find another word. Read
The Shariyat-Ki-Sugmad. If you find a word
there—perhaps *Anami* or another name which
refers to the God realm or the SUGMAD—chant
it; try it that night. See how it works.

Sometimes you get a new word on your own
before an initiation, and the ECK Initiator gives
you another word during the initiation. You
wonder which one is right. The one that you
receive on your own should always be regarded
first, because it comes from your own inner
worlds.

But it isn't by mistake or accident that you
happen to get two words. Sometimes your own
word stops working after a few weeks or months.
That's when you use the other one. Or you can
experiment: Try using both words together, or

in combination with HU, Wah Z, SUGMAD, or any of the other sacred names in the ECK teachings.

Here's another way to get a new word. First go into contemplation. Blank the mind and see which words come to the forefront of your mental screen.

When you get an initiation, you'll be told that the initiation requires a word with a certain number of syllables. Let's say the initiation you are in requires a one-syllable word. See if one of the words or thoughts or impressions that just happens to come to you can be reduced to whatever number of syllables your word should be for that initiation circle.

When you find one, try it out. Use it for about a week or two and see if it works. If it doesn't, try another one. If it still doesn't work, you can become more earnest with your Friday fasts.

93. Watching Your Dreams

The dream world and its people are real. It is only our recall and understanding of it that are incomplete. Our link with the inner worlds is usually through dreams, but illusion can make our memory of inner events faulty.

What about the dream people who appear to be just symbolic parts of ourselves? Let's start with the waking dream. The Mahanta uses it to give someone a spiritual insight from an experience in his daily life. The Master draws on the individual's experiences with real people and real events to point out some personal truth.

Apply the principle of the waking dream to your dream world. The people you meet there are Souls, just like you. However, the Mahanta can turn your experiences with them into an open window of understanding, to unlock your desires, needs, and goals.

Keep a journal of your dreams and begin to note any parallels between them.

94. How to Make Good Decisions

Everyone wants to make good decisions. But how do you know when you are being guided by the ECK or by the mind? Here's a simple way to tell.

If guided by ECK, you are more likely to change your mind when new information comes along. You're quicker to admit that an earlier decision based on sketchy information needs to change.

The mind has the power to make you believe you are always right. That's why a headstrong person acts so smart. He thinks he's always right, though he's often wrong.

95. The ECK Way to Pray

There are a lot of people who pray to God in the wrong way. They want others to do things their way, so they use prayer to control others and bring about their own wishes. It's like a basketball team praying together before a game: "Dear God, help us win." Meanwhile, on the opposite side of the court the other guys are busy doing the same thing. What kind of prayer is that?

When you ask God for help, you can say, "I am aware of the situation and the problem, and I want your help in whatever way you see fit." This is the attitude of the ECKist. You look to see what you, yourself, can do to make the thing work; how you can overcome your own problem.

When you practice this, you are learning, unfolding, getting experience to become a mature Soul—someone fit to be a Co-worker with God.

96. Decompressing the File

Sometimes the information you receive in the dream state comes to you like a computer file that's compressed for document storage. The ECK Masters often speak to the chela with a highly compact form of communication, much like telepathy.

Imagine turning on an inner computer and putting a diskette into the disk drive. You are going to be decompressing the file of the Master's inner discourse to you. Try to keep the intent of the discourse as you convert it into everyday language. There is no word-for-word utility program that will exactly translate an inner conversation into outer words.

Sometimes this exercise is even harder than trying to keep the exact meaning of a message in English that is translated first into French, then into Spanish, then back into English again.

97. An Easy Way to Resolve Karma

If you feel burdened by karma in your life, here's an easy way to resolve some of it.

Do all deeds in the name of the Mahanta, the Living ECK Master. Perform your regular chores knowing that each is in the service of the Master. Each duty and task is done with the knowledge that it is done with love for the Master. If you sweep the floor in your house, instead of doing it out of love for the house, your family, or visitors, do it out of love for the Master.

This brings divine love into all you do. When an activity is performed with divine love, it can burn off karma and bring spiritual development. Often it is as good a means as Soul Travel itself.

Practice this exercise faithfully. You will find that life begins to teach you how to listen to the Mahanta, the Living ECK Master via the silent communication.

98. Front of the Line

Visualize yourself where you are right now, then chant HU and imagine yourself where you want to be. Do this spiritual exercise for a few minutes, putting all your attention on it. Then relax and release the situation to the Holy Spirit, the ECK.

A man in Africa used this technique when the clinic where he brought his very ill son was completely full. After four hours of waiting, he began to wonder if he'd ever get to see the doctor. His son was getting worse by the hour.

When he tried this technique, he saw himself walking with his son to the front of the long line to see the doctor. He even imagined going through the doors into the room where the doctor treated his patients.

Not long after the man began the exercise, a new doctor came into the waiting room from outside. He saw the ECKist's son lying on the sofa. The boy had just begun to sweat heavily.

Walking over to the boy, the doctor asked, "Whose son is this?" "He's my son," said the ECKist. "I'll see him right away," said the doctor. "He may be very sick."

When you do this technique with purity in your heart and release the outcome of the situation to the ECK, you can bring about great changes in your life.

99. Controlling Your Own Mind

Going after God requires you to have every mental faculty filled with ambition to achieve that goal. Never crowd your mind with trivial or unnecessary thoughts, with reading too much, with too many plans, nor with trying to do too much physically. Keep your mind clear, unhurried, and filled with the radiant form of the Living ECK Master.

If someone seems stronger willed than you and you feel pushed into something because of their strong personality or forcefulness, simply think of the Mahanta, the Living ECK Master and he will come to your aid.

The process of controlling your own mind is:

1. putting the mind completely on God, and keeping it there
2. surrendering yourself to the Mahanta, the Living ECK Master
3. controlling the vibrations

The secret to controlling the vibrations is in the feelings. It begins with having the right symbol within. Should you have the image of the Mahanta, the Living ECK Master always before your Spiritual Eye, it will bring the right mental vibrations.

If your mind is running out of control, if you are thinking negative thoughts, simply stop pushing or crowding your thoughts against the door of the mind, for they pile up badly, creating just what you are fearing. Transfer your attention to the Mahanta, the Living ECK Master, the Light and Sound within.

There will be a release of the darkness within you, and light and joy will prevail. Then you will have control of your mind and thoughts.

100. Setting Goals

First choose something you want in your life or pick a problem that needs to be dealt with. Then set clear goals.

Second, ask yourself the following questions. Your goals must pass four tests. (1) Are they specific? (2) Are they realistic? (3) Can the results be verified? and (4) Do they give a date for completion?

Next, of course, you must begin working toward your goals in your daily life. As you do this, you can also use visualization or daydreaming to help you. First picture the goal clearly— what you want to do or be in life. Then fill the picture with unbounded love, because love is the true creative force that removes all limitations.

Practically all famous or successful people in the world have done this. The ECK Masters have set the goal of God-Realization and becoming a Co-worker with God for the chela of ECK. Holding this picture with love can pull you through rough times.

101. Treatment against Fear

In order to make use of the imagination, one must become completely still. If you feel your mind and emotions churning and darting about, try this exercise to still yourself inside.

Choose a verse from *The Shariyat-Ki-Sugmad,* one that seems to fit your situation. The verses of *The Shariyat* are set in such a way that they can attune you to a higher level of consciousness. It is a good treatment against fear.

Repeat the verse over and over in your mind until you feel it become a part of yourself. You will feel your consciousness lifting and your inner worlds become still and calm. You will be able to consciously lift yourself to the point that troubles are not a part of you and you can see them objectively.

When you are able to rise above the situation into a clear area of thought—where you no longer see the parts but see the whole—then you can rearrange the parts accordingly.

102. Attention Grabbers

Spend a day or a week paying close attention to unusual incidents the ECK brings you. Things happen as the ECK guides you to take a step, to make something work out right. Anything that grabs your attention may be an aspect of the Golden-tongued Wisdom. Working with this is just a matter of awareness.

Sometimes the ECK gives you warnings. An alarm going off, for instance, might not be for the most apparent reason. It could be the ECK signaling you to be alert, be aware, be on the lookout for other things. Even a sudden birdcall may be a hint that you should be careful, hurry up, or pay attention.

The worlds of ECK in the lower regions interlock like puzzle pieces. With expanded awareness, you are able to take in more and more of these interlocking worlds of ECK, so that when something happens to you or around you, you know how it fits in and what it means to you.

103. Create a Brighter World

If you have an uncomfortable experience or dream—or one you don't understand—take it into contemplation. Begin by singing HU for a few minutes. Then rewind the dream or experience, and run it through your mind. Next, visualize a door that opens into golden sunlight. This is the Light of God.

Now take the uncomfortable experience from the darkness; take it from the silence and solitude through the open doorway where it is dissolved by the Light and Sound of God.

This exercise can get you in the habit of looking for a brighter, more creative world, where you can find more inner satisfaction. With the help of the Inner Master, the Mahanta, you are learning to take charge of your life. You are becoming the aware Soul, the creator of your own worlds.

You will suddenly find yourself outside the physical body, looking back at it in the room. Now you are ready for a short journey in the other worlds.

Chapter Ten

Soul Travel

104. The Easy Way

Just before going to bed at night concentrate your attention on the Spiritual Eye, that place between the eyebrows. Chant HU or God inwardly and silently.

Hold your attention on a black screen in the inner vision, and keep it free of any pictures if at all possible. If you need a substitute for mental pictures flashing up unwantedly, put the image of the Living ECK Master in place of them.

After a few minutes of this, you may hear a faint clicking sound in one ear or the sound of a cork popping. You will suddenly find yourself outside the physical body, looking back at it in the room. Now you are ready for a short journey in the other worlds.

There is nothing to fear, for no harm can come to you while outside the body. Although you may not know it, the Mahanta will be standing by to keep watch over your progress. After a while the Soul body will return and slide gently into the physical self with hardly more than a very light jolt.

If this is not successful the first time, try it again, for the technique works. It has worked for others.

105. Around the Room

This spiritual exercise uses the imaginative body.

Take a seat in a chair. Make yourself comfortable. Then say, "I shall go for a short walk in the Soul body." Close your eyes, and look into the Spiritual Eye in a soft, sweet, gentle way. Sing HU for a minute or two, and then imagine yourself getting up.

If I were doing this contemplation, I would say, "I will get out of the chair in the Soul body and walk in front of the table. I will become very interested in the things around me, such as the color of the tablecloth, the flowers, and the vase.

"While the physical body is still in contemplation with its eyes shut, I will walk in the imaginative body to look at the curtains. I will touch the curtains and notice how nice this beautiful yellow cloth feels."

Become curious, and decide to see what's beneath the curtain. Observe the floor beneath the curtain, and pay very close attention to every little detail.

Now go over to the door, and turn the knob. Notice what the doorknob looks like. Before you open the door, say, "On the other side I'm going to see the Inner Master." Then open the door. Sure enough, he's there, and he says, "Are you ready to go yet? Let's take a walk outside."

You and Wah Z take a walk and look at the sights along the way. Strike up a conversation with Wah Z. Don't bring up heavy spiritual subjects yet; just talk about something ordinary.

Whenever you're ready to return, say, "Wah Z, why don't we go back to my room now? I'd like to see myself sitting in the chair." Walk back to your room. Throughout this experience, try to remember to sing HU or your secret word every so often.

Open your door, walk into the room, look over at your body, and say, "I'll see you later, Wah Z. I'd better sit down in the chair and get myself together again."

Then end the spiritual exercise by returning to your chair and opening your eyes.

As you practice this, Soul is becoming used to going beyond the physical body. At first it's only imagination, but the practice of this spiritual exercise will strengthen the experience. One day you will find yourself in a higher state of consciousness exactly as you had seen yourself in your imagination.

106. A Gentle Exercise before Sleep

Try doing this spiritual exercise each evening before you go to sleep. Close your eyes, and sing HU or your secret word for five minutes.

Then just before you go to sleep, say to the Mahanta, "Please take me to the place where I can learn whatever is important for my spiritual unfoldment. Take me to a Temple of Golden Wisdom."

Or say, "Let me see what it's like to Soul Travel; you have my permission."

If you can establish the Golden Heart, which is actually the viewpoint of Soul, you'll find it easier to have inner experiences and let go of the fear. If you have fear in Soul Travel, you have fear in other things, and it's holding you back in your life.

107. Imaginative Techniques

Soul Travel occurs in two ways. One form is experienced as the apparent movement of the Soul body through the planes of time and space. It is not really movement, because Soul already exists on all planes. What seems to be movement, or travel, is simply Soul coming into agreement with fixed states and conditions that already exist in the lower worlds.

This explains the imaginative technique for Soul Travel. You imagine a scene, and you are there in the Soul body. It may feel as though you are moving along very quickly, and this is why it is perceived as travel. Actually, it is the process of changing the setting around you.

To practice this, you can take a scene from your memories and control the actions in it. For example, imagine the sea beating against a beach. Now try to see the sea as being as still as lake water. Try it on things you know by stilling or stopping actions.

You may experience a rushing sound, like wind in a tunnel, and the sensation of moving incredibly fast.

The other form of Soul Travel is the expansion of consciousness. This is closer to the state of true personal revelation or enlightenment that we are looking for in ECK.

108. A Gateway to Soul Travel

If you are interested in Soul Travel, you can try this technique tonight in the dream state. Before sleep, close your eyes and place your attention very gently on the Spiritual Eye. Then sing HU, and fill yourself with love.

This feeling of love is needed to give you the confidence to go forward into an unknown, unexplored area. One way to fill yourself with love is by calling up the warm memory of a past occasion that filled you with pure love.

Then look inwardly for the individual who is your ideal at this time—whether it is Christ or one of the ECK Masters. In a very gentle way, say, "I give you permission to take me to the place that I have earned for my greatest spiritual unfoldment." And then silently or out loud, continue to chant HU, God, or another holy word.

Try to visualize yourself walking into the inner worlds, and know that the individual who comes to meet you is a dear friend.

If it doesn't work the first time, do it again and again. The spiritual exercises are like physical exercises: before your muscles grow strong, you have to exercise them a number of times; it doesn't always happen in one try. It's quite likely that if you take up an exercise routine for thirty days, you're going to be stronger than you were at the beginning.

It's the same way with the spiritual exercises. The purpose of the Spiritual Exercises of ECK is simply to open a conduit or a channel between yourself and the Holy Spirit, which we know as the Audible Life Stream—the wave that comes from the heart of God. From the moment you begin singing HU and looking for truth in this particular way, whether you are conscious of it or not, changes are being made in you.

109. Unlocking Truth

The ECK always brings the same truth, but it comes through differently for each individual. The word given at the ECK initiations is your own key to the ECK Life Stream, but you have to try it out and work with it.

Initially you may find that the key doesn't fit properly or the lock sticks. You can work this out in your spiritual exercises by using the following creative technique.

As you chant your secret word, visualize it in the form of a key. Fit it into the lock, and open the door to the Light and Sound in the room beyond. If that doesn't work, try something else. Maybe the key is all right, but there's something wrong with the lock. Work with it, experiment, try different ways.

110. Reminder

If you wish to Soul Travel while you are asleep, remind yourself of this several times during the day. For example, say to yourself, "Tonight I will Soul Travel in my dream."

Your mind will accept ideas that are repeated more readily than ideas that are not repeated.

Visualize the kind of dream you want to have as though it were already happening. After you have pictured the dream, picture its results. Try playing a movie scene in your mind of how you will feel when you have the advice or help you seek from the Dream Master.

111. Best Sleeping Techniques for Soul Travel

There are three main steps to prepare yourself for Soul Travel in the dream state:

1. Arrange your schedule to get as much sleep as needed to be fresh in the morning.
2. For a few minutes before sleeping, read from one of the ECK books to signal your intent to pursue spiritual activity during sleep. I recommend *The Shariyat-Ki-Sugmad,* Books One or Two, or *Stranger by the River.*
3. At bedtime contemplate upon the image of the Mahanta, the Living ECK Master. In this spiritual exercise, give an invitation to the Master like this: "I welcome you into my heart as my home. Please enter it with joy."

Then go to sleep as usual, but leave the eye of Soul alert to the coming of the teacher. Look for me, because I am always with you.

112. First Landmarks of Soul Travel

One way to leave the body via Soul Travel is to lie down after dinner when you are drowsy. Plan to nap for five minutes, and watch the process of falling asleep. If you try the exercise with your spouse, agree to meet outside the body a few minutes later. Then watch carefully as your mate steps free of the physical body and enters the spiritual one in a burst of radiant light.

One always goes out of the body when he falls asleep, but it is an unconscious act. In Soul Travel, the only difference is that we are trying to get out of the body in full awareness.

The moment Soul leaves the body, It finds Itself in a blue-grey zone near the Physical Plane. This zone is an approach to the Astral Plane. The sensation of moving from the Physical to the Astral body is like slipping through a large iris of mild wind currents; this iris is the Spiritual Eye. Soul enters this neutral zone of blue-grey tones in Its Astral form, a sheath which looks like a thousand sparkling stars.

This buffer zone, or corridor, between the Physical and lower Astral planes resembles the underground silo of an enormous rocket that is perhaps two hundred feet in diameter and more than two thousand feet deep. The ceiling of this circular pocket is open and may display a brilliant canopy of white light, or you may see a night sky sprinkled with specks of twinkling stars. There may even be a pastoral scene by a river, whose waters murmur their pleasure at life.

Whatever scene is displayed in the opening of the vast ceiling, Soul is drawn toward it at a mighty speed. Most people begin to recall their dreams only after their departure from this launching zone between the two worlds, and after their arrival at a faraway destination on the Astral Plane.

113. Gazing at a Bright Object

With this technique, you get out of the physical state into a different consciousness by concentrating on a bright object like a coin.

Gaze at a bright coin which reflects the light or perhaps a small mirror which catches the light. Then begin to concentrate on going out of the body.

While concentrating, quietly repeat to yourself the affirmation: "I am leaving the body. I am going to (whatever place desired)." Do this over and over until it becomes reality.

Suddenly you will find yourself standing outside the body, viewing it.

114. Calisthenics

In this technique, sit on the floor. Close your eyes and stretch your legs out in front of you. Take a deep breath, and reach for your toes with your fingertips. Reach only as far as is comfortable; there is no benefit in straining.

At the same time, chant the word *SUGMAD* in two parts. Both syllables are long and drawn out, sung on the outgoing breath. Leaning forward, chant the first syllable, *SUG* (pronounced SOOG). Upon returning to an upright position, finish the word by chanting *MAD* (pronounced MAHD).

This exercise opens the consciousness for Soul to visit the higher worlds. It is very important that you do this first for seven repetitions, then rest briefly and do it five times more. After resting, repeat the cycle over again. Once you leave the body, you can drop the exercise.

You should never go beyond one-half hour on this exercise.

The Living ECK Master awaits you in his radiant form. He is aways here looking for his beloved follower to arrive in Soul body.

Chapter Eleven

Meeting the ECK Masters

115. Memory Test

The Inner Master once brought me into his office and picked up a photo from the desk. He was helping me improve my memory for details, a useful skill for remembering one's journeys into the Far Country. The photo was of no one I knew.

"Study his nose," he instructed me. "Can you describe any distinguishing features to me?"

There was nothing particular about the nose, but studying it more closely, I was able to isolate a triangular shape in one part of it. To the side of that was another geometric shape, an oval.

"Why don't you do that with his whole face?" he suggested.

Yet, when the Inner Master covered the man's face and asked for a verbal description from memory, I was at a loss to give one.

He had me study the photo again. Although it was immeasurably hard for me to pick up this knack, I knew the ECK Masters were experts at this sort of identification. It was a method of training the mind's recall of important information.

To improve your memory of Soul Travel journeys, you can practice this exercise using a picture of the Living ECK Master or any of the other ECK Masters.

116. Beach Walk with Rebazar

If you would like to try a Soul Travel exercise, here is an easy one that should let you meet the ECK Master Rebazar Tarzs or enjoy a short journey into the heavens of God.

Picture yourself on a beach, walking in the sand at the edge of the water. The warm waves wash about your feet, and a light spray from the ocean leaves a refreshing mist on your face. Overhead, white gulls sail silently on the wind.

Now breathe in as the incoming waves wash toward you on the beach. Then, on the outgoing breath, sing *Rebazar* (REE-bah-zahr) softly in rhythm with the waves returning to the sea. Do this exercise for twenty to thirty minutes every day. After you are skilled at this exercise, Rebazar will come and give you the wisdom of God.

If you live near the seashore, walk along the beach to get a feeling of the sounds of the ocean. Or imagine the feeling of sand under your feet, the ocean spray, and the many blue-green waters that reach the horizon. Use your impressions from the seashore in your daily Soul Travel exercise.

You may not ever see Rebazar or another ECK Master on your short Soul Travel journey, but someone is always near to lend a hand, should you need it.

At first, you may feel that you have only

met Rebazar in your imagination, but in time and with practice, you will find that he is every bit a flesh-and-blood individual, even as you are.

117. Chanting Gopal Das

Sit in an easy chair with your eyes closed, and chant the word *Gopal*. Gopal Das is one of the guardians of the Temples of Golden Wisdom. He guards the fourth section of the Shariyat-Ki-Sugmad. This is the holy book for those who follow ECKANKAR.

The word is chanted in two syllables. It is a sacred name and must be sung as *GOH*, then *pahl*.

Keep this up with a clear mind, and you will suddenly find yourself out of the body. You will be accompanied to the Temple of Golden Wisdom where you can listen to Gopal Das speak on the Shariyat-Ki-Sugmad.

118. Consultation with the Master

Visualize yourself sitting in a large room, waiting for a consultation with the Mahanta. As you wait, look about the room. Note the furniture you're sitting in and other pieces about you. There are several ECKists around you that you may recognize and chat with a bit before you are told that you can go in.

The door opens, and you see yourself go into the inner room and meet the Mahanta. You have about fifteen or twenty minutes to talk about whatever you want, before a knock will come on the door to signal that you have a few more minutes to wrap it up. Then the door will open, and someone will say, "It's been nice you could be here," and escort you out. Another person is then led into the room.

By practicing this exercise, you can arrange this private time to meet with the Mahanta on the inner planes.

119. Meeting the Light Giver

Imagine that you are walking along a path that you're very familiar with. Along one side of this walkway are lampposts topped with large globe-shaped lights. One of the lampposts has a ladder leaning against it. Go over and climb the ladder. Using the cloth and window cleaner that you brought with you, polish the glass globe very carefully, so that when the light goes on, it will shine through clearly.

Focus your attention on what you are doing, and really get into it. As you polish the globe, know that you are moving and expanding in your consciousness. Eventually a darkness will fall, because Soul is moving into areas It knows nothing about; and where there is no knowledge, there is no light. This applies only in the lower worlds as you work with Soul Travel.

As you notice that it's getting dark, an automatic sensor switches the light on. You want to use this light to guide you as you continue your walk on the path to God, but you can't very well carry a lamppost in your hand. So what you do now is visualize the thing getting smaller and smaller, until it becomes something you can conveniently hold in your hand.

Now resume your walk. But remember, there may be things along the path, such as the wind, that will try to put out the light. It's best to be prepared for anything. Make sure your pockets are packed with extra batteries, matches, wicks, fuel, and flints—whatever your light needs. If the light goes out, don't worry about it; just relight it.

Some people like to visualize unplugging an electric cord and switching to batteries. This symbolizes letting go of the silver cord. Now you are working with a self-contained battery pack, and you can go anywhere you want. But in case the batteries run down, you can always go back to the natural elements and use flints on the material you find around.

Like attracts like and light attracts light, so just keep walking and looking for another light. Somewhere on the path you will notice an individual coming toward you, totally illuminated with a silvery white light.

As he moves nearer, you will see that it is the Light Giver, the Mahanta.

120. Dhyana Technique

The technique is simple: you gaze steadily at the shining face of the Living ECK Master on the inner screen of the mind. Keep this exercise to a half hour maximum unless you are getting results. These results should be that the Master steps into your attention and begins to lift you out of the body to start traveling into the higher worlds.

When you have your attention fixed on the Master's image, start singing his name. You can sing *Harji, Wah Z,* or simply *Z*. The Living ECK Master awaits you in his radiant form. He is always here looking for his beloved follower to arrive in Soul body.

121. Mahanta at the Door

Throughout the week, somebody is always knocking on your door or ringing your doorbell. Each time it happens, say to yourself, "It will be the Mahanta, the Living ECK Master." Be very aware of what you are doing at that moment— where you walk, what you touch, and what you see. When you open the door, no matter who it is, be conscious and aware of what the person looks like and what he or she is wearing.

Let's say you're in the kitchen washing dishes when the doorbell rings. Observe your movements. You reach for the towel, dry your hands, walk to the door, and open it up—and expect to see the Mahanta.

It might be the little child from next door, but this is the ECK in expression at a certain level. It's bringing something for you. In a sense, each being on every plane is the Mahanta; and in some way the Mahanta is expressing some degree of truth through every person we meet.

When you go to bed that night, review any experiences you had with visitors. Retrace your steps from the moment you heard the knock until the time you opened the door: The person knocked several times; you noticed this or that on the way to the door; you knew it would be the Mahanta. Who did you see when you opened the door? It was the newsboy collecting for the paper.

Remember details: What was he wearing? What did he say? This is a spiritual exercise that you can build into your daily life. Try "The Mahanta at the Door" during the day. The energy you have put into this will carry over and help you at night.

You are going to get very used to opening the door and expecting to see someone that you want to see standing there. This helps to open the heart so that you can open the door with love. Because unless you do, you will never see the Inner Master. If you can open the door with love, the Master will come to you, because the Mahanta is always there.

The spiritual exercises work best when done with goodwill, a feeling of happiness in your heart, and with joy in expectation of seeing the Mahanta.

Chapter Twelve

Troubleshooting the Spiritual Exercises of ECK

122. Traveling beyond Fear

If you feel fear when practicing Soul Travel techniques, begin your contemplation with this thought: "I love the SUGMAD with all that is within me."

What happens if you love someone or something with your whole heart? Fear is pushed out of your mind! Therefore, go into contemplation, putting a thought into your heart about something you did once that made you happier than you've ever been before.

This takes practice of course, but trust the Mahanta and chant your word. He will be near you for your protection at all times.

I hope that this will help you get over your fear. It is quite a natural thing, but you will see it growing less powerful as you keep on with your spiritual exercises.

123. A New Slant

People often get more intense with their spiritual exercises when things appear to go wrong. Why? Perhaps because they want to force something in their life to go where *they* feel it ought to go. Or, the going is more tough than they expected.

Do a spiritual exercise anyway when all goes wrong. However, do it with a new thought in mind.

Ask the Mahanta, "What is thy will?" Then chant HU and put your full attention on the problem, for the Master will show how you can grow spiritually by meeting the problem.

When you go to sleep at night, tell yourself, in a very relaxed way, "I'm not going to worry or think about the spiritual exercise. If the Inner Master wants me to have a certain experience, great; but I'm not going to be trying. I'm just going to get some rest."

Then look into the inner vision, and chant yourself to sleep. This will relax some of the tension or fear you might be feeling about Soul Travel.

For some of you a certain exercise will work. Others of you will find other ways to do your spiritual exercises. Experiment.

As you do the spiritual exercises, set up enjoyable things to do on the inner planes. If one technique doesn't work for you, then modify it, adapt it, experiment. Do whatever you can and enjoy yourself.

124. Why Keep a Journal?

When you do an exercise, keep a journal of the things you remember from your dreams and waking experiences. Even if it's just a feeling, write it down.

This helps you to develop the discipline to make it easier for Soul to work Its way through the mind and the lower bodies to bring a conscious awareness of the inner planes down to earth.

If you can remember the experience, you can work with these inner enlightenments from the Mahanta.

125. The Spirit of Love

The spiritual exercises work best when done with goodwill, a feeling of happiness in your heart, and with joy in expectation of seeing the Mahanta.

On the inner planes, the Mahanta is the representation of the SUGMAD, which is often seen in the form of the Living ECK Master. If you can fill yourself with love, you have a very good chance of being successful in Soul Travel.

How do you invoke the spirit of love? You can do it in any number of ways.

For instance, when you go into contemplation, you can put your thoughts and mind upon a past experience where you were filled with love. This will set the tone for your state of consciousness. Then begin chanting one of the secret names for God or your personal word.

You are the one who must set the tone of love and let it fill your heart. Your whole being has to be filled with love, not from the head, but from the heart. And then, as you make your preparations to go inwardly, you say to the Inner Master: "Mahanta, please take me to the place that is right and fitting for me at this time. I put myself in thy hands."

126. Listening

When you get out of the habit of listening, the voice of the Inner Master becomes weaker and weaker. Not because he is speaking in a quieter voice, but because you have turned down the volume control on the inner instrument of Soul.

There is a stream of consciousness from the mind that constantly goes through you. Chanting your word or HU keeps the stream pure. People who stop chanting or stop the spiritual exercises can all of a sudden fall into depression and negativity. They don't know why.

It happens because that stream of consciousness, the play of the mind, has become polluted.

The singing of this sacred prayer song or name of God purifies the thoughts which lead to your actions. It makes for a happier, more harmonious life.

You'll find by listening more and practicing the spiritual exercises every day that upliftment comes gradually as you are ready for it.

127. When Visualization Is Hard

No one can look closely with the inner vision. It is more a relaxed and easy sensing of the object. The inner vision does not work in the same way as our outer eyes. It goes more keenly into the object, seeing more but with less strain.

Whenever difficulties with visualization come to mind, say firmly to yourself, "I can visualize a little already, so I have only to develop what I already know."

Everyone visualizes unknowingly when looking forward to something. Until you can visualize to your satisfaction, think and feel consciously.

128. Instinctive Ability

Understand how the ECK works: If It gives you some knowledge on how to sidestep a problem and you listen, then It will give you still another insight on how to run your life even better.

On the other hand, if you get lazy, if you say, "It couldn't have meant that," and you don't act on it, the ECK—the Mahanta—will try again. But when you get out of the habit of listening, the voice of the Inner Master is harder to hear.

For this reason, I strongly encourage you to continue the Spiritual Exercises of ECK. Even when it seems they are not working, you may notice that your life is going more smoothly. When you stop the spiritual exercises, you lose the ability to know instinctively what you should do to run your life in the best way.

129. Patience and Commitment

One of the most common stumbling blocks for the new ECKist is impatience. For the more experienced ECKist, it is often commitment.

After doing the Spiritual Exercises of ECK for just two or three weeks, someone will write in and say, "I must be doing something wrong. I'm not having any experiences. My life seems to be worse than before."

Say you're going to study to be a doctor—and it's a profession worthy of putting your whole attention into for an entire lifetime. How many would expect to become a doctor or be good enough to perform intricate surgery after only two weeks?

It takes longer for some. Others have done the groundwork in other lifetimes, and they pick up the spiritual exercises more quickly.

An excuse that twenty minutes a day is too much time to spend on the Spiritual Exercises of ECK shows little self-discipline. This is like the fellow who talks of becoming a writer but gives all sorts of reasons why he does not write. The truth is, he is simply not committed to writing.

Is the ECKist committed to the expansion of consciousness?

130. Continue to Experiment

I experimented a lot with the Spiritual Exercises of ECK. I was an adventurer, a traveler. I would do a spiritual exercise the way it was described in the ECK discourse, and if it didn't work in two weeks, I'd do it a little bit differently.

Anytime a certain spiritual exercise no longer works for you, it may mean you have unfolded beyond the scope of this particular exercise or personal, secret word.

Use your creative abilities to go a step further. Find another word or another spiritual exercise, so that you can tune in to a higher level of spirituality which you have attained in the spiritual worlds.

The Mahanta, the Living ECK Master uses many different methods to try to get through your barriers or resistance. One spiritual exercise or another is tried, and then another. They approach your state of consciousness from a number of ways.

There's no need to push against the door of Soul, however. With continued practice, the spiritual exercises will begin to open your awareness, first at one level of consciousness, then at another.

131. Giving Something Back to Life

If you do the spiritual exercises and get more of the Sound and Light of Divine Spirit flowing into you, what are you going to do with it?

Mostly people just like to contemplate, enjoy the inner experiences with the Light and Sound, and sit like bumps on a log.

There is little reason to learn how to move with the expansion of consciousness unless you are going to do something with it. You can't spend your life in contemplation of the higher truths without doing anything to bring a little light to your fellowman.

One way to start is this: Simply give back some service of love to the world, your friend, your neighbor; and it may be simply by doing a good deed every day that no one ever knows about.

The farther you go in your ECK initiations, the more you will find yourself serving, helping, and being among people. You'll carry the message of the Light and Sound of God in whatever way is needed at a particular time. Sometimes you'll do this without even talking about ECK. The ways of ECK are often quiet. When you are being used as a channel, you may never know exactly what was accomplished through you.

There is no greater joy than working as a Co-worker with God. Giving something back to life when you have the ECK coming in is absolutely essential for spiritual survival.

The future will require more love, more compassion, and more understanding. Energy used in service to God and mankind is better than time spent in judgment of one another. Love is the key to spiritual freedom.

Do you want the secret of love? Then note these words from *The Shariyat-Ki-Sugmad,* Book One: "Love does not come to those who seek it, but to those who give love." Contemplate sweetly on love, and the wisdom of God shall find you.

I am always with you.

Glossary

Words set in SMALL CAPS are defined elsewhere in the Glossary.

ARAHATA. An experienced and qualified teacher for ECKANKAR classes.

CHELA. A spiritual student.

ECK. The Life Force, the Holy Spirit, or Audible Life Current which sustains all life.

ECKANKAR. Religion of the Light and Sound of God. Also known as the Ancient Science of SOUL TRAVEL. A truly spiritual religion for the individual in modern times, known as the secret path to God via dreams and SOUL TRAVEL. The teachings provide a framework for anyone to explore their own spiritual experiences. Established by Paul Twitchell, the modern-day founder, in 1965.

ECK MASTERS. Spiritual Masters who can assist and protect people in their spiritual studies and travels. The ECK Masters are from a long line of God-Realized SOULS who know the responsibility that goes with spiritual freedom.

HU. The most ancient, secret name for God. The singing of the word HU, pronounced like the word *hue,* is considered a love song to God. It is sung in the ECK Worship Service.

297

INITIATION. Earned by the ECK member through spiritual unfoldment and service to God. The initiation is a private ceremony in which the individual is linked to the Sound and Light of God.

LIVING ECK MASTER. The title of the spiritual leader of ECKANKAR. His duty is to lead SOULS back to God. The Living ECK Master can assist spiritual students physically as the Outer Master, in the dream state as the Dream Master, and in the spiritual worlds as the Inner Master. Sri Harold Klemp became the Living ECK Master in 1981.

MAHANTA. A title to describe the highest state of God Consciousness on earth, often embodied in the LIVING ECK MASTER. He is the Living Word.

PLANES. The levels of heaven, such as the Astral, Causal, Mental, Etheric, and Soul planes.

SATSANG. A class in which students of ECK study a monthly lesson from ECKANKAR.

THE SHARIYAT-KI-SUGMAD. The sacred scriptures of ECKANKAR. The scriptures are comprised of twelve volumes in the spiritual worlds. The first two were transcribed from the inner PLANES by Paul Twitchell, modern-day founder of ECKANKAR.

SOUL. The True Self. The inner, most sacred part of each person. Soul exists before birth and lives on after the death of the physical body. As a spark of God, Soul can see, know, and perceive all things. It is the creative center of Its own world.

SOUL TRAVEL. The expansion of consciousness. The ability of SOUL to transcend the physical body and travel into the spiritual worlds of God. Soul Travel is taught only by the LIVING ECK MASTER. It helps people unfold spiritually and can provide proof of the existence of God and life after death.

SOUND AND LIGHT OF ECK. The Holy Spirit. The two aspects through which God appears in the lower worlds. People can experience them by looking and listening within themselves and through SOUL TRAVEL.

SPIRITUAL EXERCISES OF ECK. The daily practice of certain techniques to get us in touch with the Light and Sound of God.

SUGMAD. A sacred name for God. SUGMAD is neither masculine nor feminine; IT is the source of all life.

WAH Z. The spiritual name of Sri Harold Klemp. It means the Secret Doctrine. It is his name in the spiritual worlds.

Bibliography

Chapter One: Starting with the Spiritual Exercises of ECK

1. *Journey of Soul,* Mahanta Transcripts, Book 1.
   Be the HU.
   The Dream Master, Mahanta Transcripts, Book 8.
2. 1993 *ECKANKAR Journal.*
3. *Be the HU.*
   Unlocking the Puzzle Box, Mahanta Transcripts, Book 6.
4. Ibid.
5. *The Secret Teachings,* Mahanta Transcripts, Book 3.
6. *Soul Travelers of the Far Country.*

Chapter Two: Dream Exercises

7. *The ECK-Ynari.*
8. *The Dream Master,* Mahanta Transcripts, Book 8.
9. Ibid.
10. *The Mystic World,* Summer 1985.
    Cloak of Consciousness, Mahanta Transcripts, Book 5.
11. *Letter of Light,* Winter 1987.
12. *The ECK-Ynari.*
    The ECK-Vidya, Ancient Science of Prophecy.
13. *The ECK-Ynari.*
14. *The Book of ECK Parables,* Volume One.
    The ECK-Vidya, Ancient Science of Prophecy.
15. *The Book of ECK Parables,* Volume 3.
16. *The Living Word.*
17. Ibid.
18. *The Golden Heart,* Mahanta Transcripts, Book 4.
19. *Cloak of Consciousness,* Mahanta Transcripts, Book 5.
20. *The ECK-Vidya, Ancient Science of Prophecy.*
    The ECK-Ynari.
21. *The Golden Heart,* Mahanta Transcripts, Book 4.

Bibliography

Chapter Three: Healing and Protection

22. *The Secret Teachings,* Mahanta Transcripts, Book 3.
23. *The Mystic World,* Winter 1983.
24. *The Book of ECK Parables,* Volume 3.
25. *Dialogues with the Master.*
26. *Cloak of Consciousness,* Mahanta Transcripts, Book 5.
    Soul Travelers of the Far Country.
27. *The Secret Teachings,* Mahanta Transcripts, Book 3.
28. *The Living Word.*
29. *The Book of ECK Parables,* Volume One.
    The Golden Heart, Mahanta Transcripts, Book 4.
30. *Cloak of Consciousness,* Mahanta Transcripts, Book 5.
31. *ECKANKAR: The Illuminated Way Letters.*
32. *Cloak of Consciousness,* Mahanta Transcripts, Book 5.
33. *The Golden Heart,* Mahanta Transcripts, Book 4.
34. *Letters to Gail,* Volume III.
35. *The Book of ECK Parables,* Volume 3.
36. *The Book of ECK Parables,* Volume One.
    The Golden Heart, Mahanta Transcripts, Book 4.

Chapter Four: Exercises for Balance and Healing

37. *Cloak of Consciousness,* Mahanta Transcripts, Book 5.
    Soul Travelers of the Far Country.
38. *The Golden Heart,* Mahanta Transcripts, Book 4.
39. *The Secret Teachings,* Mahanta Transcripts, Book 3.
40. *Cloak of Consciousness,* Mahanta Transcripts, Book 5.
    Letter of Light, Spring 1989.
41. *The Secret Teachings,* Mahanta Transcripts, Book 3.
42. *The Shariyat-Ki-Sugmad,* Book Two.
43. Ibid.
44. *Earth to God, Come In Please . . .*
45. *Unlocking the Puzzle Box,* Mahanta Transcripts, Book 6.
46. *The Golden Heart,* Mahanta Transcripts, Book 4.
    Letter of Light, Spring 1987.
47. *Cloak of Consciousness,* Mahanta Transcripts, Book 5.
48. *The Book of ECK Parables,* Volume 3.
    The Shariyat-Ki-Sugmad, Book Two.

Chapter Five: Solving Problems

49. *Soul Travelers of the Far Country.*
50. *The Secret Teachings,* Mahanta Transcripts, Book 3.
51. *The Book of ECK Parables,* Volume 2.
52. *Letters to Gail,* Volume I.
53. *The Flute of God.*
    The Secret Teachings, Mahanta Transcripts, Book 3.
54. *Letters to Gail,* Volume III.
55. *The Book of ECK Parables,* Volume 2.
56. Ibid.
57. *The Secret Teachings,* Mahanta Transcripts, Book 3.
    Cloak of Consciousness, Mahanta Transcripts, Book 5.
58. *The Secret Teachings,* Mahanta Transcripts, Book 3.
59. *Cloak of Consciousness,* Mahanta Transcripts, Book 5.
60. *The Mystic World,* September–October 1982.

Chapter Six: The Light and Sound of God

61. *Journey of Soul,* Mahanta Transcripts, Book 1.
62. *The Golden Heart,* Mahanta Transcripts, Book 4.
63. *Cloak of Consciousness,* Mahanta Transcripts, Book 5.
64. *Child in the Wilderness.*
65. *The Spiritual Notebook.*
66. *The Secret Teachings,* Mahanta Transcripts, Book 3.
    Cloak of Consciousness, Mahanta Transcripts, Book 5.
67. *The Spiritual Notebook.*
68. *The Golden Heart,* Mahanta Transcripts, Book 4.
    Letter of Light, Fall 1989.
    Unlocking the Puzzle Box, Mahanta Transcripts, Book 6.
69. *The Living Word.*
70. *ECKANKAR: Compiled Writings,* Volume 1.
    The Book of ECK Parables, Volume 2.
71. *Unlocking the Puzzle Box,* Mahanta Transcripts, Book 6.
72. *Stranger by the River.*

Chapter Seven: Self-Discipline

73. "Peanut's Hard Road to Freedom," 1992 ECK Summer Festival, Anaheim, California, June 14, 1992.
74. *The Book of ECK Parables,* Volume 3.

75. Ibid.
76. *Cloak of Consciousness,* Mahanta Transcripts, Book 5.
77. "The Light and Sound Are All Around," 1992 ECK European Seminar, Paris, France, July 25, 1992.
78. *Letter of Light,* Spring 1986.
79. *The Mystic World,* September–October 1982.
80. *The Shariyat-Ki-Sugmad,* Book One.

Chapter Eight: Open-Eyed Techniques

81. *Cloak of Consciousness,* Mahanta Transcripts, Book 5.
82. *Letters to Gail,* Volume I.
83. *How to Find God,* Mahanta Transcripts, Book 2.
    The Mystic World, Spring 1992.
84. *The Mystic World,* Fall 1985.
85. *Letters to Gail,* Volume III.
86. *Letter of Light,* Fall 1991.
87. *The Book of ECK Parables,* Volume One.
88. *Cloak of Consciousness,* Mahanta Transcripts, Book 5.
89. *The Living Word.*
90. *Soul Travelers of the Far Country.*
91. *How to Find God,* Mahanta Transcripts, Book 2.

Chapter Nine: Mastering Your Fate

92. *How to Find God,* Mahanta Transcripts, Book 2.
    Cloak of Consciousness, Mahanta Transcripts, Book 5.
93. *Letter of Light,* Fall 1990.
94. *Letter of Light,* Summer 1990.
95. *The Secret Teachings,* Mahanta Transcripts, Book 3.
96. *Letter of Light,* Summer 1990.
97. *ECKANKAR: Illuminated Way Letters.*
98. *The Book of ECK Parables,* Volume 3.
99. *Dialogues with the Master.*
100. *Letter of Light,* Spring 1985.
    Letter of Light, Spring 1986.
101. *Letters to Gail,* Volume I.
102. *Cloak of Consciousness,* Mahanta Transcripts, Book 5.
103. *The Book of ECK Parables,* Volume 3.
    The Dream Master, Mahanta Transcripts, Book 8.

Chapter Ten: Soul Travel

104. *In My Soul I Am Free.*
105. *The Secret Teachings,* Mahanta Transcripts, Book 3.
106. Ibid.
    The Golden Heart, Mahanta Transcripts, Book 4.
107. Ibid.
    Letters to Gail, Volume III.
108. *The Golden Heart,* Mahanta Transcripts, Book 4.
109. *Cloak of Consciousness,* Mahanta Transcripts, Book 5.
110. *The ECK-Ynari.*
111. *Letter of Light,* Winter 1986.
112. *Soul Travelers of the Far Country.*
113. *ECKANKAR—The Key to Secret Worlds.*
114. Ibid.

Chapter Eleven: Meeting the ECK Masters

115. *Soul Travelers of the Far Country.*
116. Ibid.
117. *ECKANKAR—The Key to Secret Worlds.*
118. *The Book of ECK Parables,* Volume 2.
119. *Cloak of Consciousness,* Mahanta Transcripts, Book 5.
120. *The Spiritual Notebook.*
121. *The Golden Heart,* Mahanta Transcripts, Book 4.

Chapter Twelve: Troubleshooting the Spiritual Exercises of ECK

122. *ECK Youth Newsletter,* Summer 1984.
123. *Letter of Light,* Fall 1991.
    The Secret Teachings, Mahanta Transcripts, Book 3.
124. *The Golden Heart,* Mahanta Transcripts, Book 4.
125. Ibid.
126. *The Book of ECK Parables,* Volume 2.
    Journey of Soul, Mahanta Transcripts, Book 1.
127. *The Flute of God.*
128. *The Golden Heart,* Mahanta Transcripts, Book 4.
129. *Journey of Soul,* Mahanta Transcripts, Book 1.
    The Living Word.

Bibliography

130. *Journey of Soul,* Mahanta Transcripts, Book 1.
The Golden Heart, Mahanta Transcripts, Book 4.
131. *How to Find God,* Mahanta Transcripts, Book 2.
Unlocking the Puzzle Box, Mahanta Transcripts, Book 6.
The H.I. Letter, Winter 1989.
The H.I. Letter, Spring 1991.

How to Learn More about ECKANKAR
Religion of the Light and Sound of God

Why are you as important to God as any famous head of state, priest, minister, or saint that ever lived?

- Do you know God's purpose in your life?
- Why does God's Will seem so unpredictable?
- Why do you talk to God, but practice no one religion?

ECKANKAR can show you why special attention from God is neither random nor reserved for the few known saints. But it is for every individual. It is for anyone who opens himself to Divine Spirit, the Light and Sound of God.

People want to know the secrets of life and death. In response to this need Sri Harold Klemp, today's spiritual leader of ECKANKAR, and Paul Twitchell, its modern-day founder, have written a series of monthly discourses that give specialized Spiritual Exercises of ECK. They can lead Soul in a direct way to God.

Those who wish to study ECKANKAR can receive these special monthly discourses which give clear, simple instructions for these spiritual exercises.

Membership in ECKANKAR Includes

1. The opportunity to gain wisdom, charity, and spiritual freedom.
2. Twelve monthly discourses which include information on Soul, the spiritual meaning of dreams, Soul Travel techniques, and ways to establish a personal relationship with Divine Spirit. You may study them alone at home or in a class with others.
3. The *Mystic World,* a quarterly newsletter with a Wisdom Note and articles by the Living ECK Master. In it are also letters and articles from members of ECKANKAR around the world.
4. Special mailings to keep you informed of upcoming ECKANKAR seminars and activities worldwide, new study materials available from ECKANKAR, and more.
5. The opportunity to attend ECK Satsang classes and book discussions with others in your community.
6. Initiation eligibility.
7. Attendance at certain meetings for members of ECKANKAR at ECK seminars.

How to Find Out More

To request membership in ECKANKAR using your credit card (or for a free booklet on membership) call (612) 544-0066, weekdays, between 8:00 a.m. and 5:00 p.m., central time. Or write to: ECKANKAR, Att: Information, P.O. Box 27300, Minneapolis, MN 55427 U.S.A.

Introductory Books on ECKANKAR

ECKANKAR—Ancient Wisdom for Today

Are you one of the millions who have heard God speak to you through a profound spiritual experience? This introductory book will show you how dreams, Soul Travel, and experiences with past lives are ways God speaks to you. You can begin to recognize yourself as a spiritual being.

Soul Travelers of the Far Country

By Harold Klemp

Harold Klemp tells the fascinating story of how he became the Mahanta, the Living ECK Master, a spiritual leader for our time. He introduces you to the ancient secrets of other ECK Masters, Soul travelers he met along the way.

Earth to God, Come In Please . . .

Stories from ordinary people who have become aware of a greater force operating in their lives. Their experiences outside the commonplace brought lessons in love and spiritual freedom that changed them deeply. They show how we can make contact with the Voice of God, for spiritual knowledge and awareness beyond words.

HU: A Love Song to God

(Audiocassette)

Learn how to sing an ancient name for God, HU (pronounced like the word *hue*). A wonderful introduction to ECKANKAR, this two-tape set is designed to help listeners of any religious or philosophical background benefit from the gifts of the Holy Spirit. It includes an explanation of the HU, stories about how Divine Spirit works in daily life, and exercises to uplift you spiritually.

For fastest service, phone (612) 544-0066 weekdays between 8:00 a.m. and 5:00 p.m., central time, to request books using your credit card, or look under **ECKANKAR** in your phone book for an ECKANKAR Center near you. Or write: **ECKANKAR, Att: Information, P.O. Box 27300, Minneapolis, MN 55427 U.S.A.**

There May Be an
ECKANKAR Study Group near You

ECKANKAR offers a variety of local and international activities for the spiritual seeker. With hundreds of study groups worldwide, ECKANKAR is near you! Many areas have ECKANKAR Centers where you can browse through the books in a quiet, unpressured environment, talk with others who share an interest in this ancient teaching, and attend beginning discussion classes on how to gain the attributes of Soul: wisdom, power, love, and freedom.

Around the world, ECKANKAR study groups offer special one-day or weekend seminars on the basic teachings of ECKANKAR. Check your phone book under **ECKANKAR**, or call **(612) 544-0066** for membership information and the location of the ECKANKAR Center or study group nearest you. Or write **ECKANKAR, Att: Information, P.O. Box 27300, Minneapolis, MN 55427 U.S.A.**

☐ Please send me information on the nearest ECKANKAR discussion or study group in my area.

☐ Please send me more information about membership in ECKANKAR, which includes a twelve-month spiritual study.

Please type or print clearly   940

Name _____

Street _____ Apt. # _____

City _____ State/Prov. _____

Zip/Postal Code _____ Country _____